I Heart My Little A-Holes

Karen Alpert

ISBN: 0-615-87338-3
ISBN 13: 978-0-615-87338-1

Dedicated to Zoey and Holden. I write about the bad stuff because it's funnier and because there's so much good stuff it wouldn't fit in a book. I love you both more than you can possibly imagine.

CONTENTS

THE TRUTH, THE WHOLE TRUTH, AND NONE OF THE BULLSHIT YOU SEE ON PINTEREST 151

THIS IS A REALLY SHORT CHAPTER ABOUT GIRL SCOUT COOKIES BECAUSE GIRL SCOUT COOKIES ARE SO F'ING AWESOME THEY DESERVE THEIR OWN CHAPTER 179

DISNEY AND CAILLOU AND OTHER ANNOYING CRAP I WANT TO CRAP ON 187

INTRODUCTION

This is my book. Thanks for reading it. Yeah, I could say more, but who the hell wants to read an introduction? Okay, now that that's out of the way, let's begin this shit with a bang.

5 Funny Stories About Vajayjays

FOR THE LOVE OF GOD, LADY, IT'S A LOCKER ROOM NOT A NUDIST COLONY

So the other day I'm sitting in the locker room at the gym leaning over to tie my shoelaces when I look up and BAM, there's a big ole giant vajayjay in my face. I shit you not. Less than a ruler's length away from my eyes is someone else's hoo-ha. The last time I was this close to a vajayjay, I was coming out of my mother. And just to paint you a picture, imagine if Carrot Top never got a haircut. Yeah, like that. So two things go through my head:

A.   Have you never heard of a towel?
B.   Have you never heard of a razor?

The truth is I have no problem with a hairy bush but you need to cover that shit up. Even Adam and Eve wore fig leaves and they were the only two people on earth. I mean they were bumping uglies (apparently a lot considering what they started) but they were still covering up their shit. So anyways, why the hell do locker rooms make people think it's okay to walk around naked?!!! I know what some of you are thinking right now.

EXHIBITIONIST NUDISTS: It's a locker room. Why on earth should we have to cover up in a locker room?

ME: Because I don't know you. You are a stranger. We have never met before. Why in God's name should you be showing me your vagina?!

I apologize for using the real "V" word (insert heebie-jeebies emoticon here). But these nudists don't use words like vajayjay and hoo-ha and I need to speak their language when I talk to them. I know a few of you are glad I used the word vagina and are totally annoyed when I use words like vajayjay/hoo-ha/pink taco/yoni/bearded clam/coochie/Rumpled Slit Skin. Kidding, I have *never* used the phrase Rumpled Slit Skin. I don't know why, but the word vagina just bothers me for some reason. Oh yeah, because it sounds gross.

Anyways, as I'm sitting there in the locker room with front row tickets I didn't buy to someone else's vajayjay, this is what I look like:

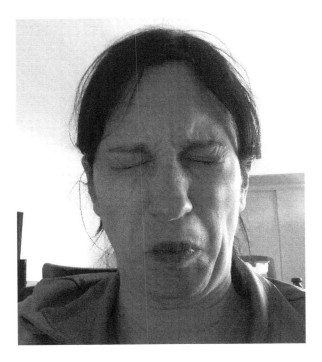

And she's blocking me in and I'm totally stuck in the corner and my Zumba class is about to begin, which really doesn't matter to me because I hate that class because I can't dance worth shit but still I don't feel like being blocked in by a vajayjay. As a claustrophobe and a vagiphobe, this is like my worst nightmare EVER. I can't even say excuse me because my mouth is filled with throw up that I haven't managed to swallow yet, so I hug the lockers like I'm Tom Cruise on an eighty-story building in Mission Impossible and I slide out around her. I swear to God if a single pube touches me, I'm going to scream and cry like I'm on fire.

But guess what I'm faced with as soon as I get around her. Like three other giant vajayjays. There are vajayjays everywhere I look. Agggghhhh, I have got to get out of here! As I'm running through the locker room avoiding hoo-has like they're landmines, I almost bump smack into this chick who has a towel wrapped around her waist (thank God) but is completely topless while she dries her hair. Just because your boobs are small doesn't mean they're invisible, lady.

Half-naked hair drying lady is the last straw, so I close my eyes tight and put my hands out in front of me so I don't crash into any walls and I run for my life. "Dear God, please don't let me accidentally grab any breasts," I think as I blindly bolt toward the exit with my hands out in front of me.

After what seems like an eternity, I'm finally safe and sound out of the locker room and in my Zumba class trying to catch my breath and find an empty spot near the back of the room where no one will see me dancing. Of course about three minutes later guess who's standing in the front of the room. Vagina lady number one. Of course. Big bush ladies always pick the front row because they have no shame and they like to show off their shit. Well, at least she's facing forward and I'll be staring at her ass and not her camel toe the whole class.

Anyways, you know how the gym is. It always sucks motivating to get there but you feel awesome afterwards. Yeahhh, not so much this time. But that night getting undressed, I guess I kinda sorta feel like a tiny bit better about my own bush. Even though it's February and I haven't groomed it in like five months, it's not like I haven't groomed it in, uhhh, I don't know, forever.

You say vagina,
I say vajayjay,
You say penis,
I say peeper,
Vagina, vajayjay,
Penis, peeper,
Let's call the whole thing off.

I'D LIKE THE BRAZILIAN
IN THE BACK PLEASE

A few days ago I'm reading some funny stuff on the Internet when I stumble upon this TOTALLY AWESOME picture. And while I'm supposed to be doing a million different things, all I can think is there's no F'ing way I can pass by vajayjay cupcakes without writing something right away. So here goes. A few thoughts I had about these beauties:

Totally awesome pussycakes made by Amy Clites, Created by Chance, www.CreatedbyChance.blogspot.com

1. I have never ever had a single desire to lick vajayjay. Until now.

2. I do believe the only proper way to eat this is to lick the frosting off first. Slowly. With a lot of tongue. And look someone in the eye while you're doing it.

3. I mean at first I'm thinking these would be like so perfect for a lesbian party. But then I realize, nooooo, these could like totally ruin a lesbian forever. "Ummm, I'm sorry sweetie, ever since I ate that chocolate hoo-ha, yours just tastes a little off or something."

4. Or I could be totally wrong. I'm not a lesbian so I don't know. Maybe it's actually the *cupcake* that's disappointing. "Blagggh, WHAT IS THIS? Chocolate?! I was expecting that awesome vagina flavor." Kind of like when you think you're biting into a grape but it's an olive. Yuck.

5. I'm sitting in Panera right now and I've got this picture like *really* big on my screen and there's a table of old men sitting behind me and whispering. I'm so tempted to turn around and shout, "Hey, quit staring at my vaginas!"

6. Well, I'm usually into black girls, but I kinda want a vanilla one. Is that racist?

7. I wonder if Martha Stewart has ever whipped up a batch of these. I can only imagine how beautiful her frosted vaginas would be. "I used a mirror to look at myself and make sure I was adding just the perfect amount of food coloring to tint it a beautiful pussy pink."

8. Mmmm, these are soooo moist.

9. WOMAN: Want to split one with me?

   FRIEND: Sure, pass me a knife and I'll give it an episiotomy.

10. Dear lady who baked these,

There better be cream in the center. Otherwise, it's just gonna leave me unsatisfied.

11. I am so tempted to bring a batch of these to my next gynie appointment to hand out to everyone. Why thank you doctor, yes I would like my speculum warmed.

12. You know that cake for Mardis Gras that has that little plastic baby inside? I kind of think these should have that too. Holy crap, there's a baby in my vajayjay!

13. All in favor of Channing Tatum eating one of these in slow motion, say aye!

14. Hey, if you're not gonna eat your clit, can I have it?

Dear Thomas the Train creators,

Did you seriously have to name one of the trains Percy? Because how the F am I supposed to keep a straight face when my toddler keeps saying "I love Pussy" over and over again?

Sincerely,
A mom with her mind in the gutter

MATH-TERBATING
AND LABIA MAJORAS
(you're either very enticed or
very turned off right now)

I have two distinct memories of my vajayjay in childhood. Here they are.

The year was 1981 and my friend Ariel and I were sitting in third grade Math class. FYI, her name isn't really Ariel (no one was named Ariel until 1989 when the Little Mermaid came out), but I always change my friends' names to keep them anonymous. Especially when I'm telling a story about their vajayjay.

So we were sitting in Math class and Mrs. Lincoln was busy writing something on the chalkboard, so my friend Ariel decided this was the perfect time to teach me an important life lesson.

ARIEL: Hey, if you scoot all the way over on your chair, you can rub on your chair like this and it feels really good.

ME: Like this?

ARIEL: No, further, so you're half on, half off.

ME: Like this?

But I didn't really need to ask because suddenly I knew exactly what she was talking about. 8 + 8 = Oh yeahhhhh.

POCAHONTAS: What are you guys doing?

ARIEL: This.

And Ariel demonstrated to Pocahontas. And then Jasmine. And then Belle. And then Mulan. Until all the girls in Math class knew exactly how to rub their hoo-has on their chairs and get off. By the time Mrs. Lincoln turned back around, all ten girls were stealthily math-terbating. And by stealthily I mean obviously.

Can you imagine what it must have been like to turn around from the chalkboard and see ten girls all leaning to one side of their chairs rocking back and forth on their crotches trying to mask their looks of ecstasy? I mean Mrs. Lincoln probably had to stifle her laughter for the next twenty minutes until she could finally escape into the teacher's lounge.

Anyways, you know how it is—gotta pay it forward. So I decided to teach my friend Cinderella a little sumpin' sumpin' she could do with her sumpin' sumpin'.

It happened when we were at her house getting changed into our leotards for ballet class. Today's lesson: how to stand naked in front of a mirror and pulled down your labia majoras (or as I call it, the regular skin on your vagina) so they look like cow udders. FYI, I totally had to Google labia majora because I couldn't remember what it's called and now my eyes are scarred for life from all the pictures I saw. So yes, if you pull down your labia majoras you can make your vajayjay look like a cow udder. Of course not once you're older and have hair there. Not that I've tried it, but I'm guessing.

You know what cracks me up the most about this? Can you imagine turning around to see your friend pulling down her vagina skin to make it look like cow udders? I'd be like uhhhh, yeah, we're not friends anymore. But at eight-years-old this just solidified Cinderella's and my friendship even more. We spent the next twenty minutes dancing around the bedroom naked and singing, "Look at me, I'm a cow! I'm a cow! Mooooooooo!" And continued to do it every week as we got ready together for ballet class. I mean does that shit ever get old?

And this is when I pray this book doesn't sell very much and no one reads this entry.

Note to self: Make sure daughter is wearing underpants before she lifts her leg to show Grandma her tattoo on Skype.

YOU CAN LOVE YOUR PAGINA, JUST DON'T *LOVE* YOUR PAGINA

You'd think my daughter would have discovered her orifices years ago. I mean my son was checking out his peeper as soon as his tiny hand could handle his massive package. Kidding. His dinky is as dinky as all the other babies'. But one day, look out.

Anyways, my daughter is three now and all of the sudden every time I turn around her finger is up one of her nostrils. Now I don't care what other people think (total lie) but I do care about all the boogers she keeps handing me. Agggh, can you pleeeease be normal and eat it or wipe it on the furniture or something?!

But her newfound orifice obsession gets worse. Her nostril isn't the only hole she's taken an interest in lately. Yeahhh, you know what's comin'. The other day I walked into her bedroom to find her sitting naked on the floor (better than the other places I've found her sitting naked— the sprinkler, her bike, her brother's head), and she's checking out things down yonder when we have the following conversation.

ZOEY: (totally melodramatic) I'm a little sad because there's a hole in my tushie.

ME: You mean your vagina?

ZOEY: Yeah, my pagina.

ME: (trying to keep a straight face) Everyone has a hole there. Where would you pee from if you didn't have that? (and do other shit we're not going to discuss)

ZOEY: It would come out of my mouth. I'd lean over the toilet and the pee would come out.

Ummm, uhhhh, I don't even know where to begin. Maybe we should talk about all of the things that are *right* with this conversation because all of the things that are wrong with it would take up the next 50 pages.

But seriously, how do I tell her to stop checking out her pagina? Telling her to stop picking her nose is a no-brainer. I mean basically I tell her to stop and she just hides under the covers and does it.

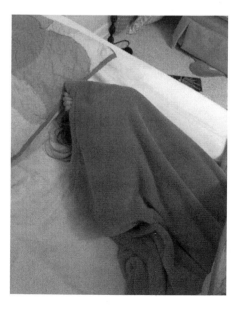

Whatever, if I can't see what you're doing and you're not killing anyone, have a ball, kiddo.

But if I tell her to stop playing with the beaver, who knows what long-term effects it will have. Will she think her pagina is taboo? Will she be too scared to touch it one day? Will she rebel and do it all the time? Gasp, like me in Math class?!! It's no easy task, but I need to teach her to love her pagina, just not to *love* her pagina. At least not yet. WTF, did I seriously just write that? I had no idea some the things that would come out of my mouth as a parent. But not pee pee. Thank God there's another hole for that.

Duh, of course babies scream their heads off when they're born. Wouldn't you cry if you had to travel head first through your mom's vagina?

I'M GONNA WASH THAT GRAY RIGHT OUT OF MY PUBES

Tis the season to let your bush grow. But the other day my friend invited me over for a Girls' Night Out in her hot tub and she invited me like five days in advance so there would be plenty of time to lawn-mow my bikini line. Usually she invites me at the last minute which means I don't have enough time to groom "down under" (shout out to all the Australians reading this!) so I make the ladies close their eyes while I'm getting in and out of the hot tub. You think I'm kidding but I am not. I have good friends who are willing to do this for me, and I know that none of them have peeked yet because none of them have thrown up or turned to stone.

You see, basically I don't have a bikini line. I have hair shorts. I mean they're not like hair Bermudas or anything, but if I don't shave it looks like I'm wearing Daisy Dukes that are made of hair. FYI, please do not write me a letter that you are so thankful you are NOT one of these people and that God/genetics gave you wonderful blonde hair in all the right places and none of the wrong places. And if you feel the need to say shit like this to me, please include your return address so I can come kick your ass. And steal your bush so I can have it surgically implanted on my hoo-ha.

Anyways, while the kiddos were napping I locked myself in the bath-room (as opposed to what? When they're not napping and I lock myself in the bathroom?), and I lined up all of my instruments on the counter. Razor, tweezers, sticky wax sheet thingies I found once at Walgreens and have never been able to find again, an electronic device that spins really quickly and rips the hair out (nahhhh, it's not painful if I imbibe the right mix of vodka and Oxycontin) and a lawnmower. And then I started the painstaking process of grooming my bearded clam.

About halfway through, this happened.

ME: Aggggggghhhhhhhh! WTF is that?!

Holy shit, my midlife crisis was finally legit. OMG, OMG, OMG, I tried to remember the breathing techniques I once learned in baby class, but I hadn't paid much attention because I was too busy laughing at words like vagina and anus. As I sat there in my bathroom looking down, I realized that one of my worst fears had come true. There he was. A little rat bastard standing there staring me right in the face. A gray pube. A mother F'ing curly little gray pube.

And if you're wondering why I'd get so hung up on one measly little hair, I'll tell you why. Because do you know how horny gray hairs are? They're like F'ing bunnies. You go to sleep and when you wake up they've multiplied. I know this from the ones on my head. I fully expect to have a totally gray bush in the next two months.

But I gotta wonder, when they come in "down there," how will they come in? Will they be haphazardly scattered throughout the field? Or will they come in on the sides in gray patches like Mitt Romney's sideburns? Or maybe there will be one gray streak down the middle like Stacy London on *What not to Wear.*

STACY LONDON: I tell you what, honey— that gray hair on your pink taco is what not to wear.

But alas, does it really matter how it comes in? The bottom line is that one day soon the carpet will not match the drapes. Like Samantha said in Sex and the City, "I have AARPussy." I usually don't like to steal other people's shit, but there's no better name for it. My pussy is officially on the *do not resuscitate* list.

I'm F'ed. Or maybe I'm not anymore.

A LOT OF SHIT YOU DON'T NEED
WHEN YOU'RE HAVING A BABY

So you've just walked into Babies R Us for the first time ever and one of the employees (who either had a lobotomy or needs one) hands you this little booklet that has a list of alllllllllllll the shit you're going to need for the upcoming arrival of your little poop machine.

And that's where the fun begins. And by fun I mean the crazy torture of going up and down each and every aisle trying to figure out whether you need F'ing nipple shields or Butt paste. The correct answer is yes and yes.

With that said, man did we buy a lot of crap for Baby #1. Baby #2, on the other hand, got all hand-me-downs. Yup, every single little thing. Yes, even the diapers. And no they weren't cloth. I don't care how good cloth diapers are for the environment, there ain't no way I'm putting turds into my washing machine. Not that there's anything wrong with that. Except for the fact that you're putting turds into your washing machine. But I digress.

So here goes. A bunch of shit I bought when I was having a baby that I now know was a total waste:

1. A fancy bedding set
Like two seconds after you tear open your fancy bedding package a BabyCenter email appears in your inbox. Ding! Bumpers killed

9 million babies last year (FYI, I like to exaggerate, it was only like 7 million). Okay then, no problemo, you just won't use the bumpers. And then you're reading your *What to Expect* book and it tells you what to expect in the first year: expect your baby to die if you put a blanket in his crib. Okay then, you'll just throw the quilt on the back of the nursing chair for decoration, which totally doesn't work because then your head is all shoved forward when you sit in the chair. So basically you've just spent a bazillion dollars on a single fitted crib sheet. A single sheet that is about to be destroyed when your newborn poops his brains out the first night home from the hospital. And I don't care how much Shout you use, that shit stain ain't coming out. So you have two choices. A. Don't buy the totally adorable bedding set to begin with. Or B. Buy a set with a lovely brown amoeba pattern all over it so the shit stains blend in.

2. Clothes that go over a newborn's head

Have you ever tried to put clothes on a newborn? F'ing impossible. You're all like my new baby has a really strong neck until you're pulling that really cute onesie over her head to take her home from the hospital and suddenly her neck is like Jello and her head falls off and you're screaming, "NURSE NURSE!" and she's walking in all cool and collected like they see this shit all the time. Well, at least that cute leopard-print onesie with the Burberry trim is soooo adorable maybe no one will notice that your child is headless.

3. A wipes warmer

Yeahhh, that's what you want to do, let baby get used to having his royal ass cleaned with a wipe that's been heated to the perfect temperature. 'Cause then do you know what happens? You're out in public trying to change his diaper and he throws a conniption because your wipes in the diaper bag are freezing and his ass has turned into a total pussy (wait, that's not right). Besides, do you think someone like the Fonz had warm wipes when he was a tike (tyke?)? No way, no how. Because people who have warm wipes as infants turn into douchebags. No, I don't have any examples, but it seems pretty damn obvious. So unless your Mum is Kate F'ing Middleton, no one's heating your stupid wipes.

4. Shoes for your newborn

Newsflash, babies can't walk. Plus, if you stare really hard at your baby's feet you can literally see them growing, kind of like how if you stare really hard at a clock without blinking you can see the minute hand moving. So basically putting a newborn's growing feet in shoes is akin to Chinese foot binding. Yes, I know those two-inch Air Jordans are like the cutest things in the whole wide world but maybe I forgot to mention, BABIES CAN'T WALK much less dunk a basketball. Except maybe those roller-skating Evian babies.

5. Expensive baby clothes

This one's pretty much the same as the last part of #1. Just buy a lot of cheap shit from Tarjay or once again, buy everything with a brown amoeba pattern on it.

6. A fancy stroller

If you're the kind of person who bought your house outright without a mortgage, I hate you. Wait, no, that's not what I meant to say. If you're that kind of person, by all means, buy a fancy delancy stroller. I remember standing in the middle of a high-end toy store while a woman half my size demonstrated the Bugabooger to me. "Push this button, then this one and voila it's so compact it fits in the palm of your hand." And then I remember this. Standing in the middle of the F'ing parking lot at Scabies R Us and I couldn't get my damn fancy stroller to collapse because it had like 9,000 doodads and buttons and levers and thingamajigs.

These days I'm like just give me a simple umbrella stroller, and if I want something fancier I'll buy it for half the price on Craigslist. You know, in case I decide to chuck it across the parking lot and then drive over it with my minivan.

7. A baby bathtub

Guess what, your house already came with one. WHAT?! The realtor didn't tell you?!! Hello braniac, it's called a sink. But wait, my sink doesn't look like a cute whale or a duck! No, it doesn't. But it also doesn't cost an extra $30. Or come in a weird ass shape that doesn't fit in any logical place in your bathroom. And guess what, your kiddo's not thinking, "It's not fair, Javier down the street has a bathtub that looks like a turtle and I don't." All he's thinking is, "Aggghhh, who the fuck is pouring goddamn water on my head?! I'm gonna scream as loud as humanly possible until they stop!"

8. Car seats

I mean, WTF is it with everyone getting these things?! Nahhhh, just kidding. Seriously, I'm kidding. Awww, shit, how many people just read this and stopped reading because they hate me now? Definitely buy a car seat.

9. The Bumbo seat

There are all these companies out there that make stupid products to help your kid hit some milestone they're gonna hit anyway, like the Bumbo. In case you don't know, this is a little seat that props your kid up before he can actually sit up on his own. You're gonna hear all these jackasses, I mean really nice moms, say that their kiddo wasn't sitting up and then she got him the Bumbo and whatta you know, two weeks later the kid was sitting up. All because of this magic chair. Ennhhh, wrong. Your kid is sitting up now because he's two weeks older. Not because

27

you forced him to use his Bumbo and work his muscles into a damn six-pack. Who do you think you are, Jillian Michaels?

10. Pee pee teepees

FYI, pee pee teepees are just a cute present people buy because their gift only came to $15 and they needed a $5 item to make it expensive enough. Oh, and they're always people who never had a boy so they have no idea that pee pee teepees don't stay on, but of course, you never realize it's fallen off until your kid starts spraying you with urine and some of it gets in your mouth.

Are you F'ing kidding me? You wake up screaming at 3:15 in the morning and need to be rocked back to sleep for like thirty minutes, but you can fall asleep in downward dog or whatever the F yoga pose this is right before lunch? Kid, you're cute, but you suck.

OH DEAR LORD, WTF IS THAT?

How did you find out you were preggers? Most people pee on a stick and wait for it to show two blue lines, but the second blue line has to be as dark or darker than the first, and the longer you stare at it the more you wonder whether it really is darker or whether your mind is just playing tricks on you. That's the way I found out the first time when I was preggers with Zoey. But not the second.

There I was standing in my closet when suddenly I noticed something. That's weird, my boobs are leaking. Got milk? Yup! All I needed now were some Oreo cookies. I know you're probably thinking, "Big whoop, my boobs gushed like Old Faithful when I was breastfeeding." But here's the thing. I had stopped breastfeeding Zoey over eight months ago. Eight months!!! So why the hell were my nipples leaking?

As I was standing their staring at my leaky boobs wondering whether I needed to call an F'ing plumber, I had a guess about what might be going on. And then four positive pregnancy tests later, I was positive. Yup, I was preggers. And what a weird-ass pregnancy symptom, right? Leaky boobs.

Sometimes I hear feminists call God a She and I'm like dude, I am all for equal rights and equal pay, but there is no F'ing way God is a woman with all the shit our bodies go through when we're preggers. No woman would design us this way. Like sometimes I think if God has a wife, she's probably like are you F'ing kidding me, G? WTH were you thinking? I mean, finally I have the rack I've always wanted but it doubles as a vending machine for this little poop machine (gesturing to Jesus). And my sense of smell is like so bionic I can smell Saint Peter's breath from two clouds away and he clearly had banana peppers for lunch. And what's up with the constipation? I've been sitting on the porcelain throne all day to squeeze out a miniscule rabbit turd. WTH were you thinking when you created this body?

But I digress. At least it's a religious digression, though, right?

So lay it on me, what's your weirdest pregnancy symptom? That strange dark facemask thing? Cankles? A swollen vajayjay? 'Cause guess what, I've got you beat. Nope, not the leaky boobs. Weirder than that.

Back when I was preggers for the first time with Zoey, I was showering one day when I noticed a little bump on my porno-sized boobs. Not a lump. A bump. But being the crazy hypochondriac I am, I was positive it was cancer so I wrote it on my mile-long list of shit to talk about with the doctor when I saw her. She didn't seem too alarmed, but she sent me to a dermatologist "just in case." Translation: it's probably cancer and you're going to die and leave your clueless husband all alone to care for this little rug rat all by himself.

As I waited on the exam table in my sexy paper gown, I prayed it wasn't cancer and that it was a clogged pore or a keloid, whatever the F that is. But nothing could prepare me to hear the two words that actually came out of the doctor's mouth when he examined the bump.

DOCTOR: Supernumerary nipple.

ME: Come again?

DOCTOR: A supernumerary nipple.

Uhhhhh, WTF? Did I hear him correctly? I think my shocked/embarrassed/confused/about-to-blow-chunks look made him explain further.

DOCTOR: Sometimes these things happen to pregnant women. It's nothing to worry about. Just an accessory nipple.

Are you F'ing kidding me? Nothing to worry about? Earrings, purses, headbands—now these are accessories a girl can appreciate. But no one walks into Bloomies and says, "Excuse me, but I'm looking for a nice third nipple." I mean WTH was I supposed to do with this thing? Embrace it? Get it pierced? Slap some pasties on it? Too bad they only come in two packs. At least I assume they do. I've never actually bought pasties so I'm just guessing.

Anyways, as much as I HATED my thripple, eventually I learned to appreciate it. When I gave birth and it went the F away.

Wanna know what it feels like to have a hemorrhoid? Go get a grape and put it in your tush hole. Now leave it there and walk around with it all day. Wait, and put some Tabasco on it before you put it there so it burns. Welcome to hemorrhoidville.

Welcome to Hemorrhoidville
Pop. 17

JUST CONNECT A TO B AND N TO J AND L TO R AND V TO F AND K TO G AND J TO Q AND Q TO B, AND THAT'S HOW YOU PUT A BREAST PUMP TOGETHER

Dear Medela,

So it's been three months since I had my baby and here's the shit that's gone through my head in the past two minutes. Is it hot in here? Where did I leave my keys? Wait, no, where did I leave the baby? Who the hell turned down the temperature in here? Agggh, I am seriously going to kill my husband, like for realz this time. I can't remember what my birthday is. Shit, is it hot in here? I think I might have just been sleeping standing up. OMG, did I just answer the door with my top off? Whatta we live in an F'ing igloo? It's freezing in here.

In case you don't get what I'm saying, I'm saying that my hormones are bouncing off the walls like they're in an F'ing pinball machine that's being played by a kid with ADHD and a roll full of quarters. My point is this.

This is pretty much what your Medela breast pump looks like online:

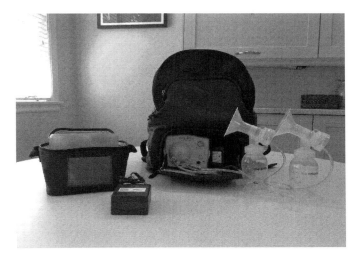

And here's what it actually looks like when it arrives and you open it up:

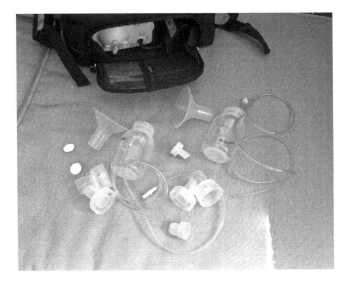

And here's how you put it together:

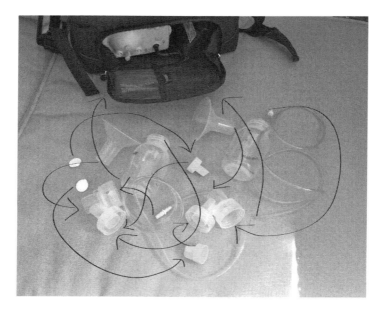

I remember opening mine up about a month before I had to go back to work, taking one look at all those tubes and doodads and valves, and breaking down into a pile of tears and snot. Thank God my husband was home to scrape me off the floor.

HUBBY: Let's tackle this later, okay honey?

ME: (sobbing uncontrollably) Nooooo, she's going to starve to death if I don't start pumping RIGHT NOW.

So here's my request. Can you pleeeeeeease start packaging the pumps assembled? Is it really that difficult? I mean I know that personally I will never forget how to put a breast pump together, but there are thousands of hormonal women who are going to open up their breast pumps for the first time tomorrow and they're either going to give up on breastfeeding or they are going to murder someone. Maybe their husband. Maybe their baby. Maybe some poor unsuspecting soul who's walking below their building when they chuck the whole damn breast pump over the balcony.

Yours truly,
Baby Sideburns

Sometimes I give my kid the finger through the baby monitor for all the shit she put me through that day. It just makes me feel better.

CHUGGA CHUGGA TYPHOID

Before I had kids I had no F'ing idea how many times I would have to take them to the doctor's office. I mean, you go to the doctor once a year, right? Well, twice. Once to your regular one, and once to the one with the stirrups. Giddy up.

But apparently babies need to go like 9,000 times a year. And that's just for wellness checkups. Which they're always F'ing well for. And then the second you get them home they're like pulling at their ear or barfing up their spleen or some shit like that and you're dragging them back to Flutopia because they caught something when they were there for their wellness checkup. It's a vicious cycle.

Anyways, here are a few things I think about the pediatrician's (holy crap is that a hard word to type) office:

1. Okay, so imagine yourself ordering a cup of coffee from the barista at Starbucks and they're all nice to you and smiling and they hand you your coffee and then out of nowhere they stab you with a needle. That's basically what it's like to get shots when you're a baby. Two nurses come in and they're super sweet and smiling at you and wearing cute outfits with smiling bears or some shit like that and then since you have absolutely no F'ing clue what's about to happen because you were just born, all of the sudden from out of nowhere they jab you with needles. In order to prepare the baby for what's coming, I think

it'd be so much better if the nurses would come in like total assholes and yelling and stuff and then jam needles into the baby's limbs. "ROOOOOAAAARRR, we're gonna stab you with BIG F'ing needles and it's going to hurt like a bitch!!!" At least then the baby would be expecting something bad to happen.

2.   If I didn't love my pediatrician so much, I'd change doctor's offices. Why? Because of this:

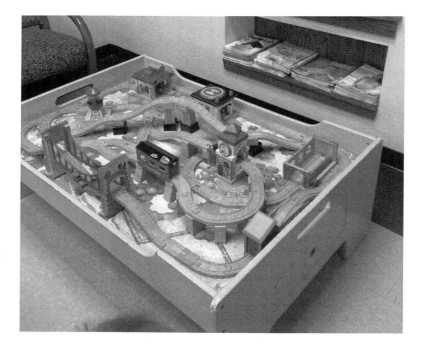

I call it the Ebola train table. Oh here's a good idea. Let's let every sick little rug rat who comes through here play with this thing and put their saliva fingers all over it so that my kid can come in next and chew-chew on it and catch the plague.

Brilliant. All aboard the Hot Zone! We came here with a minor cold and we're leaving with typhoid. Awesome.

3.   RECEPTIONIST: Northwest Pediatrics, how can I help you?

ME: Hi, my kid is coughing up a lung and I need to get him in to see Dr. Smarty Pants today.

RECEPTIONIST: She can see him at 1:30 PM.

ME: Do you have any other times? That's like smack in the middle of his naptime.

RECEPTIONIST: Ummm, yes, she can see him at 1:32 PM.

ME: Thank you, that's much better.

Not.

4.   Holden, don't touch the fish tank. Holden, don't tap on the fish tank. Holden, don't put your mouth on the fish tank. WTF? I know you're a toddler but can't you just stand there in the middle of the floor and not touch a thing and look at the fish from a distance for 18 minutes while we wait for your name to be called? I'm so glad I drove here like a bat out of hell to make our appointment time.

5.   NURSE: So the doctor will be in soon.

ME: So should I keep his clothes off?

NURSE: Yes, the doctor will be in soon.

ME: Define soon. Like four minutes?

NURSE: Soon.

ME: Thirty minutes? I just want to know if I should dress him so he's not cold.

NURSE: The doctor will be in soon.

ME: Agggggh, ANSWER ME DAMN IT!!! I'm going to fucking kill you!!! When the hell is she going to be in here?!!!

NURSE: The doctor will be in…

ME: Don't you dare say it.

NURSE: Soon.

6.   NURSE: We're going to need a urine sample from your daughter.

ME: Okay, then you better just follow her around all day holding a cup under her naked hoo-ha because A. Getting her to pee on demand is impossible and B. She can't even hit the toilet half the time and that cup's like 1/10th the size of the toilet bowl.

7.   DOCTOR: Sooo, is he saying any words yet?

ME: Yeah, lots. Honey, what does a cat say?

HOLDEN: (Blank stare)

ME: What does a cat say?

HOLDEN: (Blank stare)

ME: Who am I?

HOLDEN: (Blank stare)

ME: He says a lot. Really, I'm not lying.

DOCTOR: (writing something on the chart) Nooo, of course not.

8. So has he had any bowel movements or flatulance out of his anus that is located right behind his penis and scrotum? Nahhh, I know that's not *really* what the doctor says but she's always using anatomically correct lingo so that's what it F'ing sounds like and I have to keep a straight face and not laugh at all and even say some of these words back to her pretending like I don't usually use words like vajayjay and peeper and toot-monster.

9. DOCTOR: Do you have any other concerns or questions about your baby?

ME: Uhhh, so my husband has a concern that I promised I'd ask you about.

DOCTOR: I think I know what you're going to ask.

ME: Okay, what?

DOCTOR: No, you go ahead.

ME: No, you say it.

DOCTOR: No, you say it.

ME: No, you say it.

DOCTOR: No, you say it.

ME: Okay, let's say it at the same time.

DOCTOR: 1, 2, 3, go.

ME: Is it normal that his penis is so small? Hey, you didn't say it.

DOCTOR: It's a rite of passage.

Of course, none of this conversation really happened this way. I mean my husband did insist that I ask if it's normal for his dinky to be so dinky. So I did. In the most clumsy, foolish, bumbling way that I could because I'm not allowed to use words like dinky to the doctor. And then I died of embarrassment.

The End. Yes, there was a number 10, but like I said, I died. Plus, I'm lazy and the Bachelorette is about to start.

I don't think it's a coincidence that my baby's eyes glow like the devil's on the video monitor. He thinks we can't see him and he's like "Muahahahahaha, I don't have to conceal my real identity now!"

WHERE THE HELL DID THE NAME BABY SIDEBURNS COME FROM?

Every day people ask me why my blog is called Baby Sideburns. Well, not every day, but every week. Hmmm, no, maybe more like every month. Okay, so what is that, like twelve people? Hey twelve people who care, this story is for you.

Once upon a time there was a blog called Mommyhood Unplugged. Isn't that like the most boringest name you've ever heard? Plus it's like ridiculously uncatchy. I'm allowed to say that because it was my blog. Then one day a friend of mine was nice enough to tell me that my blog was funny but the name of it sucked. And I was like okay, you're right, but I'm totally uncreative so WTF should I name it? Well, I had just written the following post so she suggested I call it Baby Sideburns. Yes, someone else came up with the name. So Lauren Schifferdecker (isn't that like the most fun last name to say?! I'm sitting here in Starbucks saying it over and over again and people are looking at me funny), this chapter is for you. You came up with the name Baby Sideburns. You F'ing rock. So here goes, the original post that inspired the name Baby Sideburns:

Every pregnant mom says the same thing—all I care about is that my baby is healthy. Ennhhh, wrong, I'm calling bullshit on this. You see, I'm preggers right now and there are lots of other things I worry about. Like will my baby have one of those giant red birthmarks smack in the middle of its face? Will it be born with teeth (yes, there are little vampire babies born with chompers)? And will it get my Sasquatch gene and be insanely hairy?

I was lucky the first time I gave birth because my firstborn is like this totally svelte, strawberry blonde girl who takes after her father 100%. Wait, no, 99%.

RANDOM STRANGER: She looks just like her daddy.

ME: Yeah, but she got my genitalia!

Of course, that always ended in uncomfortable silence so I stopped saying it. But I digress. Anyways, they always say the firstborn looks just like the daddy and the second one looks like the mommy so I am scared to death this baby inside me is going to come out looking like me. Not only will it be the sadly-neglected second child, IT will most likely look like Cousin It.

I was one of those babies who were born with hair on their shoulders. I shit you not. I vaguely remember the labor nurse yelling, "Quick, get me some hot wax STAT!" I mean if I don't pluck my eyebrows every other day, I start looking like Burt from Sesame Street. I'm dreading the day Zoey gets older and asks if she can do shit like get her ears pierced and braid my leg hair. But anyways, I'll get to my point.

So today we're going in to get our big ultrasound to find out whether we're having a boy or a girl. Well, really it's to find out if all of its organs are where they're supposed to be and shit, but what I most want to know is can I use all of those adorable little precious girl outfits we spent like a gazillion dollars on or do I have to go out and buy all new clothes for this little rug rat? I mean yeah the kidneys are important but there are some super cute dresses that still have the tags on them.

So anyways, since my life basically consists of thousands of post-it notes with things I can't forget, I've gone ahead and written a post-it note with a bunch of questions to ask the ultrasound tech.

1. Is it a boy or a girl?
2. How 'bout them organs?
3. Does this baby have sideburns? A mustache? A hair sweater?

So to all of you parents with cue ball babies who want to punch strangers when they say shit like, "Awwww, isn't he so handsome?" and you're like, "Yo jackass, do you think I would dress my BOY head-to-toe in hot pink?" Wait, was that a full sentence? I'm not sure but it was really long so I'm putting a period on the end of it and starting a new one. Anyways, to all of you, count your blessings. That was me with Baby #1. This round I'm scared shitless I'm going to have to call Blue Cross to beg them to cover laser hair removal.

My son is still sleeping right now (or dead???) so tonight I will attempt to do exactly what I did last night to make this happen again.

We will eat dinner at exactly 5:27 and be done at 5:43.
He will have three chicken nuggets and 16 lima beans.
He will drink from his Cars sippy cup with the purple lid.
I will do the laundry today so he can wear his zoo pajamas again.
I will read half of Goodnight Moon.
I will sing Row Row Row your boat three times and the ABCs once.
And I will place his blanket on his left side with the logo at his feet.

And I will cross my fingers. No, wait, I didn't do that last night so I won't do that.

THE SERIOUS CHAPTER,
LIKE SERIOUSLY

This chapter is not funny. No, I'm not kidding. Like if you think I'm joking, please just jump to the next chapter. I'm serious. But hey, by now you probably need a little break from laughing, right? Hopefully. Maybe. Shit, what if this book isn't funny? Okay, well, at least this chapter isn't supposed to be. No, F that, in case this book isn't funny, the whole book wasn't meant to be. Okay, back to the very serious, not-funny-at-all subject at hand.

So I have something to tell you. Something I have never told to anyone. ANYONE. Not even my husband. Especially not my husband. Like seriously, he's reading this for the first time here. And honey, if you really are reading my book, you're a stud and I love you and please start throwing away your little slivers of soap in the shower so I don't have to.

Anyways, this thing I'm going to tell you about happened within the first two weeks of bringing Zoey home from the hospital when I was in total and complete love with her. I remember sitting there not being able to take my eyes off her as I watched her being a helpless blob that did nothing at all. And yet somehow she was the most beautiful thing I had ever laid (lay??? lain??) my eyes on. Look, her finger just twitched in her sleep, awwwwww.

But in the middle of all that love there was this moment I still can't believe. I was sitting on the couch and I looked over at my two-week-old baby and suddenly this wave of emotion came over me. It was oppressive. All I could think when I looked at that tiny little being was what the fuck did I do? Not WTF. This was a full on WHAT THE FUCK. And then a thought crept into my head that to this day is so unbelievable to me. I tried to push it back down but it was too late. It was there.

Let me rewind a bit. Before Zoey came around, Greg and I had this perfect life. We had like this totally awesome marriage and the kind of life people envy. We both had good jobs. We ate dinner out and shared a good bottle of wine practically every night. On weekends we would cuddle in bed until nine or ten or whenever we felt like getting up, and then we would run along the Charles River or meet friends for brunch or go to a Red Sox game. We just did what we wanted, when we wanted, and we were crazy happy.

And then Zoey came along. And everything changed. I'm not saying in a bad way. Just in a very very different way.

As I sat there on the couch that day and my hormones felt like they were on the tilt-a-whirl at an amusement park, and it felt like red ants were eating my nipples from the inside out, and my belly still looked preggers spilling over the top of my *fatter* pants because my fat pants were no longer fat enough, as all this happened, I stared at this tiny little being and for a brief moment I thought— shit, I can't even type it. That's how bad it is. Nope, I've committed. Okay here goes. For a brief moment, I actually thought about throwing that tiny little baby off our balcony.

Gasp! Yes, there it is. That's how F'ed up I was after giving birth. Was it postpartum depression? I don't know. Is it possible to have postpartum depression for like five minutes? I mean for the most part I was over-the-moon in love with this little being. But suddenly it occurred to me that she was F'ing up everything. Did we still go out to dinner every night? Yes. But I spent like the entire meal struggling to figure out how to breastfeed Zoey without my Boppy under my Hooter Hider in front of fifty strangers as I watched my husband drink his glass of wine that I couldn't have because I was petrified of trying to piece together the 2,000 parts of my breast pump.

So that's why for a brief moment an image flashed through my mind. An image of me taking her out to the balcony and heaving her tiny little body over the railing. How absolutely horrible is that?

Did I really mean it? No, not really. Of course not. I never would have actually done it. But for a brief itty-bitty tiny moment I actually thought life might have been better if we decided to never have a child.

And suddenly I understood how moms everywhere are struggling with postpartum depression. Imagine feeling like that for an extended period of time. How awful. Suddenly I saw an itsy-bitsy glimpse of what Susan Smith must have been feeling when she drove her poor little babies into that water.

And then just as soon as the horrible image popped into my head, I pushed it out. It was a thought I had but didn't mean. You've had those thoughts before, right? What if I jump off this balcony, or drive my car over the median, or just start screaming at the cashier who won't stop talking to the person in front of me, or something else totally rash that I would never actually do? Or maybe I'm the only one who ever has these kinds of thoughts. But probably not. What I've learned the most from writing my blog is that I am *never* the only one to think the way

I do. I post something and think awww shit, what if nobody relates to this? And then like 50 seconds later, 200 of you are like yeahhh me too! So if there's one thing you get from this book (besides wet underpants hopefully. Wow, that sounds so wrong), know that you are never alone. No matter how wrong, how depressing, or how criminal your thoughts sometimes are, you are not the only person having them. But I digress. Like big time. Back to my very serious story.

So after dismissing my evil thought of throwing my baby over the balcony, like five minutes later she woke up. And I was dancing around the room singing along to Yellow Submarine holding her and looking into her little eyes and being ridiculously grateful that Greg and I made her. And I have never had a thought like that again. Ever.

YO BABY BOOK, YOU CAN TAKE YOUR MILESTONES AND SHOVE THEM UP YOUR YOU-KNOW-WHAT

Have you ever looked at someone else's kid and compared them to your own kid? And if you say no you're lying. I love when I'm sitting in Gymboree or some other place that's touched by a thousand feet and I see some asshole mom coaxing her rug rat to show off some new skill so everyone can feel like shit that their own poop machine isn't walking on their F'ing hands yet or speaking in iambic pentameter.

Like there's this father in our hemp weaving class (fake class name so this dipshit won't know I'm talking about him in case he's reading this) who's constantly saying stuff like, "People can't believe he's only one." That's because he's not, jackass. He's 19 months. This is why people speak in months when it comes to baby's ages. But even if he *were* only one, shut the F up. You're just making other parents worry and feel like crap.

And it kills me to watch some of the moms freak out when their kiddo is like the last one to talk or walk or go wee-wee on the potty. Is something wrong? Sure, sometimes there is, and that sucks balls. But usually they're fine and just taking a little longer to master some skill. I know it sucks, but someone has to be last.

And I think my favorite thing about the assholes who brag about how advanced their kids are is that milestones actually SUCK. Most milestones make a parent's life harder. So why brag about it? "Woo-hoo, my kid won't sit still on a blanket anymore so I have to watch him like 24 hours a day!" So here we go. Ten milestones that SUCK ASS BIGTIME (FYI, I know bigtime is actually two words, but I don't think it should be):

1. Eating solids

So the doctor finally tells you to go ahead and try solids with your newborn, and you're like hip hip hooray when really you should be like awwww shit, really? Because there's nothing easier than just feeding your baby breast milk. I mean I know breastfeeding hurts like a mother-F'er at first, but once you've got it down it's like the easiest thing in the world. You're at the mall and baby's hungry. Just pop out a boob and lunch is served. And formula is almost as easy. But feeding your baby baby food is basically the same thing as putting a bunch of crap in your blender and forgetting to put on the top before you flip the switch. Suddenly your kitchen looks like a fugly 1980's sweatshirt that's been splatter-painted with diarrhea green peas.

2. Saying mama

Mama mama mama mama mama mama mama mama mama mama mama mama mama mama mama mama mama mama mama mama mama mama mama mama mama mama mama mama mama! Guess what my little rug rat can say now. The first time you hear it, your heart melts a little. The second time you hear it, your eyes well up. The 918,009,576th time you hear it, you want to stab your eardrums out with an ice pick.

3. Dressing herself

As I'm standing there begging my kid to hold onto my shoulders and not my head as I help her pull on her pants, I dream of the day when she can dress herself. And then it happens. Ohhh myyyy Goddddd, it's like watching paint dry.

ME: Hello, is this the Guinness Book of World Records?

MAN: Yes?

ME: Can you please send someone to my house because I am literally watching the slowest person EVER to get dressed in the history of the world?

And don't even get me started on shoes. They're Velcro! They accidentally get stuck to everything so how F'ing hard can it be to close them?! By the time she gets them on for school she'll have to take them off again because it's time for bed. In the year 2025.

4. Potty training

I remember all the jackasses, uhh, I mean nice people, asking me if my daughter was potty-trained yet. Ummm, seriously? 'Cause either she's wearing a diaper or my three-year-old literally has Kim Kardashian's ass inside her jeggings. WTF's the hurry to potty train? I mean, don't get me wrong. I hate changing diapers. But you know what I hate even more? Waiting for the F'ing seatbelt light to go off on the airplane because my kiddo told me the moment we pulled away from the gate that she has to go potty. Or how about this? When we pull out of the driveway and we're like forty seconds down the road and she's like, "Mom, I have to pee pee!" Uhh, no you don't. You HAD to pee pee. And now you're sitting in a puddle of urine in your car seat. Awesome. I miss diapers.

5. This milestone doesn't have a name

So my son hit like the worst F'ing milestone EVER the other day. We're hanging out in the kitchen (translation: I'm on a munchies binge) when I steal a piece of chocolate from my secret stash which is on a high up shelf so I can't easily get to it, which basically means I have to drag a chair over and risk breaking bones every time I want a piece. Totally worth it and not a deterrent at all (FYI, I had to spell deterrent like four times before I got it right). Anyways, I'm standing on this chair and Holden is looking up at me screaming, "Cookie, cookie, cookie." How the F does he even know I'm getting a dessert? He's never had any. Yeah, I know "noticing when mom takes chocolate" isn't in the stupid baby book, but it should be because it's like the suckiest, most life-altering milestone ever.

6. Talking

MOM #1: My child is saying ball, truck, balloon, milk and mama.

MOM #2: Mine is saying wawa, dog, night-night, sissy and bubble.

ME: Mine is saying shit, fuck, damn, crap, and douchebag.

Yeah, learning to talk is so overrated. Remember that kid in Old School who they were always saying *earmuffs* to so he'd cover his ears when the adults were saying something R-rated? That doesn't F'ing work. I tried it. As soon as your kid starts talking, it's time to start a swear jar. Or in my case a swear wine barrel. In every fucking (I can't say it, but I can type it all I fucking want) room.

7. Moving

Ahhh, remember the good ole days when you could literally put your baby anywhere and they wouldn't move. Like I could put her on the top of a telephone pole and walk away and not worry. And then one day she rolled over and I was like awww shit, how am I supposed to shower if I can't lay her in the middle of the bed anymore? And then one day she crawled, and the "experts" said to get on all fours at her level to crawl around and look for safety hazards in your house. Cord, cord, outlet, standing lamp, glass coffee table, surge protector, cabinet full of plastic bags, outlet. Okay then, this seems safe. Not. And then one day she walked and even though the baby book says, "Date baby first walked _____ ," what it should say is, "Date mommy was F'ed _____ ."

So if you're one of those mommies whose baby isn't walking yet and some other mom comes up to you and rubs it in your face that her rug rat is, here's what I want you to do. I want you to say, "I am so sorry, your life must totally suck now." And then I want you to tell them that Baby Sideburns told them to F off.

8. Reading
Okay, so I'm finally seeing a positive side to illiteracy. Here's what one of Zoey's books says: Once upon a time Rapunzel lived in the tallest tower of Mother Gothel's castle. And here's what I read to her: Once Rapunzel lived.

My kid has no idea what really happens in the story because I basically paraphrase every single page. Which means I'm totally F'ed when she can finally read and she's like, "Mommy, you skipped that paragraph."

Okay, so I know I promised ten milestones that suck and I've only done eight, but guess who just woke up early from his nap. Numero doso. And I've already left him crying in his crib for like fifteen minutes. God help me when he graduates to a bed and can get up whenever he wants, which was going to be milestone #9 in this post. And #10 was "being able to open doors." This is how it was all supposed to end:

So now he can open doorknobs. And that's when my kiddo walked in on me having sex. With myself. Ruh-roh.

I Heart
My Little
A-Holes

ZOEY: *(holding a tampon she found) Mommy, what's this?*

ME: *It's something for mommies.*

ZOEY: *But what is it?*

ME: *A tampon.*

ZOEY: *But what do you do with it?*

ME: *It's for mommies.*

ZOEY: *But what do mommies do with it?*

ME: *They put it inside them?*

ZOEY: *Like they eat it?*

ME: *No, they don't eat it. They put it in their vaginas (sorry, I have to use anatomically correct words with her).*

ZOEY: *Like a thermometer?*

ME: *Ummm, yeah, like that. Now get in the car.*

IT'S ALL FUN AND GAMES UNTIL SOMEONE SHITS A BRICK IN THE MIDDLE OF THE RESTAURANT

ME: Hey Zoey, where do you want to go for your birthday dinner? Noodles and Company? P.F. Chang's?

ZOEY: Rainforest Café!

WTF WTF WTF was I thinking?! It's not WHERE do you want to go. It's do you want to go HERE or HERE.

ME: What about McDonald's? Or Go Roma, honey?

ZOEY: No, Rainforest Café.

Are you kidding me, seriously kid? Yeah, let's pay like $8,000 for a stupid grilled cheese you're not gonna eat and a tall brown dessert that looks like a pile of shit with sparkler candles. Not to mention there are only like two Rainforest Cafés that aren't even remotely close to our house. One is in the city where people get shot like all the time and we'd have to sit in bumper-to-bumper rush hour traffic to get there (I lovvvve breathing in exhaust on the way to getting murdered, don't you?). And the other is in totally the opposite direction in the middle of nowhere in this suburban mall I can't stand with stores with names like Too Cool.

No, I did not make that up. It's there and it sells a lot of shit that's Too Crappy.

But it's her birthday so who the F am I to make her pick something else?

ME: Okie-dokie, Rainforest it is.

ZOEY: Yayyyyyyyyyyyyyyyyyyyyyyyyyyyyyyyyyyyyyyyyyyyyyyyyyyy!

She screams and runs around like the Tasmanian Devil for like five minutes so I'm feeling a little better now. Like this much (imagine me holding my fingers a millimeter apart). But seriously, how bad can it be? Awww shit, if you have to ask that, you're screwed. Yeah, I'll take out the glitter and glue for you because how bad can it be? Sure, I'll get a free haircut from the hairdressing school because how bad can it be? Yeah, I'll volunteer to go on the school field trip because how bad can it be taking 9 kids to a public restroom that looks like it's been splatter-painted with fecal matter? So yes, it can be bad. Very bad. Like you'll be in therapy for this for a lonnnngggg time.

So the big night comes and the hubster gets off work early for the birthday dinner and we shoehorn ourselves with the grandmas into the minivan and drive like forty minutes in crazy traffic to the stupid, uhhh I mean magical, restaurant.

SAFARI GUY: (chipper) Welcome to Rainforest Café. Follow me to your table.

ZOEY: I want to sit by the gorillas!

ME: Can we sit by the gorillas?

SAFARI GUY: Sure.

ME: But not too close to them.

SAFARI GUY: Uhhh, which one is it, lady? (he doesn't actually say this but I can tell he's thinking it)

ME: (gesturing to my toddler) I'm scared he's going to be scared of the gorillas.

So Safari Guy puts us at a table facing the gorillas but not too close to them and nowhere near the fish tank I was hoping we would sit by to put Holden in a trance and make him magically eat his food and not bother me so I could actually eat dinner for the first time in twenty months. But that's okay, I'll just starve to death so my daughter can sit by some of Jane Goodall's taxidermied friends.

And then just as we're sitting down, the magic of the rainforest comes alive. Wowwww, it's amazing. The pitter-patter of rain is building, the lights start to flicker, thunder starts to boom, and the entire jungle comes alive. The birds are chirping, the gorillas are oooh-ooohahhhing, and both of my kids are shitting their pants. Holden is vicegripping my flabby neck skin and Zoey is screaming her head off.

ZOEY: Agggggh, I don't like thunderrrr! Make it stopppppp!!!

WTF, seriously kid? You picked the Rainforest Café and you don't like thunder?! It's not Forest Café. It's RAINforest Café. Yeah, I'll just go ask them if they can stop their main attraction. I'm sure none of the other customers will mind if we just skip the rainforest part tonight.

ME: Zoey, it's okay, it's just pretend. Holden, honey, they're not real.

But neither of them can hear jack shit over the sounds of the thunder and their deafening screams.

And then just as suddenly as the rainstorm started, it stops.

HUBBY: Will anyone eat the spinach and artichoke dip if I order one?

MIL: I will.

Oh thank F'ing God that's over and everything's back to normal. Only it's not because like every five minutes some elephant's trumpeting or the gorillas are shaking their fists or the thunder's booming or a butterfly's flapping its wings and my kids are having heart attacks and I'm pulling the defibrillator out of the diaper bag to revive them. Every. Five. Minutes.

And then they're fine again. And then they're shitting bricks again. And then they're fine again. And then they're shitting bricks again. And then it's back to normal again and we're taking bites of our practically inedible food, and by we I mean everyone else because I'm constantly walking Holden around to look at the fish tank we didn't get to sit next to.

And finally we finish our shitty food and four men come out and sing some weird version of happy birthday to Zoey and then the bill arrives for $19,000 and we pay it. But before we can get the hell out of there, we have to stop and listen to a talking tree because Zoey insists and it's her birthday. Side note, trees should NOT have faces because all trees with faces are scary as shit. And then we have to buy Zoey a $2,000 princess hat on the way out because it's her birthday and you know, because there are so many princesses in the rainforest. WTF?

So there you go. And we will never ever go back to the Rainforest Café. Well, not until one of the kids wants to go again for one of their birthdays.

ZOEY: Mom, I just took a picture of your tush.
ME: You're grounded forever.

THE BIG BANG THEORY

Holy shit, I just heard a giant bang in the next room. What the F was that? Here's what goes through my head:

1.   Dear God I hope that wasn't someone's head.

2.   Where's the cry? The longer the pause is before the cry, the worse it's going to be. Unless there's no cry at all and then we're F'ed because I don't remember jack shit from the CPR class I took when I was preggers with numero uno.

3.   What if it was someone's head and I didn't see it? Then I have no idea how bad it was and whether I gotta schlep the kids to the ER. And by schlep of course I mean cradle in my arms and transport them there as gently as possible.

4.   I hear laughter so WTF was that, a toy hitting the floor? Where the hell was it dropped from? The Empire State Building?

5.   Did the toy break and if so can we throw that shit away? Dear God please let it be that annoying alphabet caterpillar.

6.   You know what, never mind. Ignorance is bliss. And dinner ain't gonna cook itself so I'm staying right here with my slow cooker and my glass of vino.

GOING FROM ONE KID TO TWO IS UHHH, HOW DO I SAY THIS, LET ME SEE, HELL

So the other day we're at a restaurant and this pregnant lady with her toddler leans over from the next table and asks, "How is it having two kids?" The way I see it, I can answer her in one of three ways:

1. Thank God for Roe v. Wade, lady, because you still have a choice.
2. Here take one of mine for the day and you can see. And I get to choose which one.
3. It's nice.

Being the lazy person that I am, I go with number three, when really in my head I'm thinking, "You really want to know how it is going from one kid to two?" Read'm and weep:

1. Going anywhere sucks ass. Remember all the crap you had to carry when you had your first baby? Now multiply that times two and add another poop machine to the mix. This is when you're gonna wish you were one of those Third World country chicks who can balance baskets on her head. Yeah, you'd look like a total whack job, but who gives a shit?

2. Feeding two kids is a bitch. Just when you're all stoked because your firstborn can finally feed herself and you can go back to eating with two hands, an adorable little piranha comes along to chomp his way up your once again bleeding nips. And then when he can finally eat solids he's like, "I don't give a rat's ass if that's what my sister liked. I'm going to pick totally different shit and make you figure it out all over again." The only good news is you know how you used to cut blueberries in 16ths so your baby wouldn't choke to death? When it comes to #2, you'll slap a whole rib-eye in front of him and let him go to town.

3. Awwww, remember how nice and quiet bedtime was when you just had one child? Lying on the floor together as a family reading bedtime stories? Say adios to that shit. Because now #1 (#1 my ass) is there to help you put #2 (who #2s like a thousand times a day) to bed. Which is like putting a baby to sleep in a room full of strobe lights with a Megadeth album playing at the highest volume. ROCKABYE BABY ON THE MOTHER-F'ING TREE TOP!!!!!!!!!

4. Okay, you thought keeping one kid's hands out of the frigging tampon trashcan in the public restroom sucked when it was just her. Now you've got two little a-holes to deal with. And I mean a-holes literally. One of them's still in dipes, so you have to go back to using some nasty ass changing table that poop's touched like a thousand times, while the other kid is on the loose sucking the toilet handle (one of those broken ones that squirts water when you flush it), and there's nothing you can F'ing do about it because if you let go of the baby he'll roll off and crack his head open. Are we having fun yet?

5. We have a new rule in our house. Only one kid can cry at a time. Does it work? Hell no. If it did, I'd buy a baby on the black market and stick it with pins all the time so it'd cry and my kids wouldn't be allowed to.

6. You know how you saved all of those awesome baby toys to pass down to #2? Think again. Because as soon as #1 sees Sophie the mother-F'ing $22 giraffe that's really just a dog toy packaged in a fancy box, she and the stupid chew toy are like two goddamned lost lovers running towards each other in a field, and your second child is more like a third wheel. Nope, from now on buy two of everything. And if you can't afford two, buy cheaper shit and buy two.

7. When baby's sleeping Mommy should too. Remember that shit they told you in the hospital? Well WTF does Mommy do if they never sleep at the same time? And speaking of napping, just as your arm feels like it's going to literally fall off like you're in a Monty Python skit because your friggin' infant car seat weighs like a thousand pounds, your baby grows out of it and you're like how the F is he supposed to sleep on the go if I don't have the infant car seat anymore? So you have two choices. Stay home all day long like you're Paris Hilton on house arrest because one of your kids is always napping, or go out and about your day as one of your kids is constantly exhausted and losing his shit in public.

8. I'll bet you always thought it'd be awesome having two kiddos because they'd play with each other. Ennnhhh, wrong. They'll play with each other, in like *five* years. For the first few years, your oldest will play with your youngest like a crazy ass killer

whale plays with a seal in the surf. "Here little baby who stole Mommy and Daddy's attention from me. You know how mama and dada keep bragging about your neck muscles being so strong, why don't you come over here so I can pick you up by your head and see if they're right."

Anyways, there you go weird lady who asks loaded questions to random strangers in restaurants. I could go on and on about all the ways going from one kid to two is just awesome (insert sarcastic looking emoticon face here), but my #1 has my #2 in a princess dress and a chokehold.

April 2013

Okay, so last week I had Zoey's parent-teacher conference.

TEACHER: Blah blah blah, she plays well with others. Blah blah blah, she can be a little too sensitive. Blah blah blah, and here is her self-portrait.

I look down at the page.

WTF???

TEACHER: As you can see there is the head and the arms and the legs.

But WHAT is that between her legs?

TEACHER: And she even drew ears.

ME: No, wait, I have to stop you. What is THAT?!

Because it looks to me like my DAUGHTER drew herself a pair of balls and one of them is hairy.

TEACHER: (laughing) We don't know.

OTHER TEACHER: (laughing harder) No idea.

Fine, I'll have to take this matter into my own hands. Later that night at home...

ME: Zoey, I have a question for you.

ZOEY: Yeah?

ME: I love this drawing you did of yourself. But what's that between your legs?

ZOEY: (duh) Spiders on my tush.

Ahhh yes, I feel like such an idiot for asking.

ME: And what are the concentric circles in your head?

ZOEY: I'm screaming.

ME: (blank stare)

ZOEY: Because there are spiders on my tush.

It all makes sense now. Wait, no it doesn't. WTF WTF WTF???

1-800-KILL-ME-NOW

PRAISE THE LORD, PRAISE THE LORD, PRAISE THE LORD!
My kids are FINALLY old enough that I can let them hang out in the
other room without me! I know it may seem like a little thing, but IT
IS NOT. This means I can do shit like wash the dishes without worry-
ing that I'm going to turn around to put a bowl away and step on some
baby's head and squirt his brains all over the kitchen floor. This means
that while they're watching TV I can stealthily duck into the kitchen to
squirt some Hershey's syrup into my mouth when I need a chocolate fix.
This means I can put in my tampon without two rug rats sitting front
row and breaking out the popcorn to watch.

So the other day I was surfing porn in the living room while the kids
were in the kitchen having their snack (I just said that to sound cool.
Really I was probably shopping on Zappos), and I heard them giggling
in there.

A loud bang = get the F in there fast
Silence = get the F in there fast
Giggling = take your time and check out the heels section

So after about ten more minutes on Zappos (translation: $230, but in
my defense I will probably return it all because all I wear anymore are
ugly flats) I decided I should pretend to be a good mom and see what they
were up to. La la la la laaaa, going into the kitchen. Holy mother of God
what the fuck happened in here??!!! What sucks is since my kids were

there I couldn't actually say this out loud and could only just scream it in my head. I also had to restrain my middle fingers from twitching away from my tightened fists.

"What did you do?!!"

But neither of them answered me. Not with words at least. Zoey knew she was going to be killed, so she averted her eyes and wouldn't look at me. But Holden was too young to know he was going to die, so he kept laughing and showed me exactly what they had been doing. Flick. He pulled back the rubbery straw on his sippy cup and then let it go. And again and again and again. Flicking purple smoothie dots from the floor to the cabinets alllll the way across the ceiling. And judging by the way the room looked, I'd say they had done this about, oh I don't know, 2,000,000 times. Are you F'ing kidding me?

I can't tell you how much I wish I had taken a picture so I could share it with you, but I was too busy calling the suicide hotline. Eight hours later after I could finally start breathing again, all I could say was thank F'ing God for 409. And tall husbands. And laws against killing your children.

Some people see a weird child who likes to wear her coat backwards.

I see a brilliant genius who's figured out how to turn her hood into a feed bag.

Mom, can I put the strawberries in?

Yes, when it's time.

Mom, can I put the strawberries in?

Yes, hold on.

Mom, can I put the strawberries in?

Yes, in two minutes.

One. Two.

That's two seconds, not minutes.

Mom, can I put the strawberries in?

Agggghhhh, stop asking, stop asking, stop asking!

Mom, can I put the strawberries in?

Oh my God kid, I'm about to tell you where you can put the F'ing strawberries if you don't stop asking me.

(pause)

Mom, can I put the strawberries in?

The conversation ends here because this is when I killed myself.

The kiddos were just playing downstairs when I heard my daughter say, "I don't want my brother to die." I can't decide whether I should be:

1. *Really freaked out 'cause maybe she's like that redrum kid in The Shining and knows something.*

2. *Really touched because it might be the nicest thing she's ever said about him.*

3. *A little concerned that she's plotting something and she's hoping it doesn't go horribly wrong.*

THE OTHER NIGHT I DID SOMETHING
I SWORE I'D NEVER DO

Here's the thing. I could give a rat's ass if my three-year-old gets to bed on time. She can stay up until the crack of dawn for all I care. And yet at 7:29 PM I'm ready to explode like a ticking time bomb as she dilly-dallies before I read her my favorite bedtime book—*Go the Fuck to Sleep*. Congratulations Zoey, you just got into the Guinness Book of World Records for the slowest person to ever put on a pull-up.

So if I don't really care what time she goes to sleep, then why the hell am I freaking out at 7:29? Because do you know what happens at 7:31? Me time. Uninterrupted, sit on the couch, eat my ice cream and vege (vegge??? vedge??) out in front of the shittiest television I can find time.

So the other night when my daughter came out of her room and screamed, "Mommy!" at 7:42, 7:58, 8:03, 8:15 and 9:10, I was livid. Remember Glenn Close at the end of Fatal Attraction? Multiply that by 1,000 and you have me.

P.S. Please don't try to figure out my age based on my movie reference. I'm old. When the other mothers bitch to me that they're turning 30, I punch them in the face. Just inside my head of course.

And then last night happened. "I need water. My leg hurts. My book fell out of bed. I'm missing something. I want the other pillow. My skin hurts." When she came out for the six or seven-*thousandth* time, I lost my shit. Which blows when you have a one-year-old sleeping in the bedroom next door and you have to whisper and not use curse words and still seem mad as hell.

ME: (like Cujo if he spoke English) If I see your face one more time tonight, young lady, you are going to be in so much trouble I'm going to, ummm ummm, it's so bad I can't even say (translation: I have no F'ing clue).

Man, how I wish I were one of those parents who used middle names when I got mad. It's so much cooler than saying shit like "young lady." But when you're this pissed off, you say whatever pours out of your mouth. You just pray it's not the "c" word.

Anyway, barely two seconds after I shut her door did I hear it open again. No, that's a lie. It was at least thirty seconds later. Just long enough for me to get my dessert that I would now have to devour quickly so she wouldn't see it, which sucks because then I'd have to get another one later that I could take some time to appreciate. That was it. No one messes with my chocolate. She pushed me over the edge. And that's when I did what I swore I'd never do. I stormed upstairs, ripped the doorknob lock off my husband's office door, and attached it to my daughter's door. Yes, I put a lock on her door. Something I swore I'd never do.

Needless to say she was not happy. And neither was I. As I listened to her scream and cry and snot and slobber all over the place, all I could think about was what a horrible mother I am. Did I seriously just lock my daughter in her room? I'm like that evil old lady from *Flowers in the Attic*, only worse because my daughter doesn't have siblings in there to keep her company.

And then all the next day I hated myself for it. Until bedtime, when I removed the lock from her door and calmly threatened to put it back on if she came out of her room. She wasn't perfect. She came out once to complain that her cells hurt. But just once. After that she stayed in there.

Not only did I start to feel justified for my child-abusive punishment the night before, but I got to watch Masterpiece Theatre completely uninterrupted. No, that's lie. I saw about a millisecond of it when I was channel-surfing looking for Honey Boo Boo.

HUBBY: (to Zoey) Do you want to take a bath alone to-night or with Holden tomorrow night?

ZOEY: With Holden tomorrow night.

HUBBY: Awww, I love that she wants to take a bath with her little brother.

ME: Ennnhhhh, wrong. She just doesn't want to take a bath tonight. Watch. Zoey, do you want to take a bath alone tonight or tomorrow night with Satan?

ZOEY: Satan.

ME: (I told you so)

WHY TRAVELING WITH KIDS SUCKS ASS AND TOTALLY ISN'T WORTH IT BUT I STILL INSIST ON DOING IT

Does this shit even need an introduction? I mean who doesn't know that traveling with kids sucks ass? Remember back when it was awesome, before you gave birth to your poop machines? Packing was always a bit of a chore, like figuring out which summery clothes fit you since you've packed on a few (translation: ten) winter pounds, and of course you hated sitting in the airport if your flight was delayed. Wait, you mean I have nothing to do but go to a bar and get drunk while I wait for my plane? I thought THAT was a BAD thing??? WTF? I'd kill for that now.

But now that I have two little rug rats in tow, going to the airport is worse than being waterboarded. And if you think I'm wrong, you're wrong. I just saw that Zero Dark Thirty movie so I know. Traveling with two kids under the age of four is worse. Way worse.

Anyways, let's get to the good stuff, or rather the bad shit. So here goes. Ten things that suck ass about flying with kids:

1. So after a morning of hell because I had to wake the kids up two hours early (which should feel awesome because they do that to me every day), I get to the airport only to find out we

don't have seats together. "Don't worry, ma'am, we'll do our best." Do your best? So if you don't succeed, what, my 3.5-year-old daughter is going to sit in row 27 next to a child molester while I'm in row 12? I've got one word for you, American Airlines. Lawsuit. Yup, there's nothing more American than that.

2.   Okay, so you've finally made it into the airport, they've checked your IDs and you pick an X-ray line. Then some woman steps up in line behind you. ARE YOU INSANE, WOMAN?!!! Who the F chooses to go behind the four-person family with a baby because here's all the shit I have to deal with:

Putting the stroller on the belt while holding the baby, taking off the kids' coats, thanking F'ing God I don't have to remove their shoes anymore, taking our laptop out of the bag, finding our baggie of liquids, oh no wait that's our baggie of Cheerios, finding the real baggie of liquids, taking off my own goddamn shoes and wondering what disease I'm picking up by walking barefoot on the ground that 9 bazillion people have walked on today, getting the ginormous car seat to fit through the X-ray machine, getting the kids to go through the metal detector and walk towards the scary TSA guy on the other side who can't crack a smile, and dealing with the TSA lady who wants to "check" our milk which makes me wonder whether the kids should drink it after it's been swabbed and radiated (or whatever the F they do to it).

Oh, and then I have to put all our shit back together on the other side like a one-billion-piece jigsaw puzzle. Just typing this makes me have a panic attack. Worst. Experience. EVER.

3.　Holy crap, did you know that when you travel with a baby, the airlines lets you bring an extra "diaper" bag on the plane? They LET you. Yippeeee, as if carrying two kids plus alllll the shit you already have to deal with isn't enough, the airlines is like, you're so damn special we're going to give you the privilege of carrying one more F'ing thing. Oh, plus that stupid humungous (wow, I spelled that right!) stuffed animal your daughter swore to death she'd carry but now refuses to, and you soooo want to leave it behind to teach her a lesson, but it's just not worth the repercussions tonight at bedtime when she doesn't have Brownie or Whitey or Horny or whatever his name is.

4.　There are three kinds of people I never want to sit next to on a plane. A. That guy who hasn't showered in like four weeks and whose hair literally leaves a mark on his seat when he sits forward. B. That lady who's chomping at the bit to have a conversation from wheels up to wheels down and doesn't even stop talking when you close your eyes and pretend to sleep even though you're just dreaming up ways to kill yourself. And C. A family.

So as I'm walking on the plane with my kids, I'm trying to apologize to people with my eyes while their eyes are telling me, I hate your F'ing guts and for the love of God don't sit in my row. And then when you pass them you can literally feel them breathe out a sigh of relief until you sit in the row behind them, which is actually worse because sound doesn't travel sideways. It travels forward. Plus, kids are like professional experts at kicking the seat in front of them. So yes, I'm that asshole, the #1 most hated person on the plane. Totally misplaced anger because really they should hate my baby but you're not allowed to hate babies so I'm the patsy.

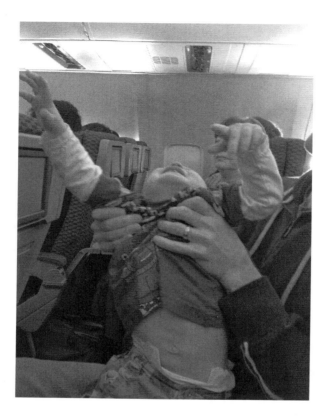

(Look at me, Mom, I'm going limp!)

5. You know what's awesome about traveling with a 16-month-old? That you don't have to pay for their ticket. You know what's not awesome? EVERY OTHER FUCKING THING. Your ticket says infant on lap, but that's a goddamn lie. Infants sit on your lap. Toddlers arch their back and pop their shoulders out of their sockets and kick you over and over again in the crotch because they don't want to be contained. You know how they won't let parents with kiddos sit in the exit row? It has nothing to do with safety. They're worried you might open the emergency door and throw your kid out.

6. The tray table. Can some airlines pleeeeeeeease invent a detachable tray table for parents traveling with kids? Because this is what kids do with a tray table. Up. Down. Up. Down. Up. Down. Up. Down. Up. Down. Up. Down. Up. Down. The whole F'ing flight. And same goes for the stupid window shade.

7. Question: What's the first thing your baby does the moment you sit down in your seat? Answer: He puts the metal part from the seatbelt in his mouth. Ohhh Mommy this feels so nice and cold on my gums. Well, kid, I hope it's worth it because you just got Ebola, avian bird flu and Typhoid all in one fell swoop. Yup, for the last two weeks I've kept you in a bubble away from every germ-infested place so you'd be healthy on our vacation, but you just canceled all that out in about two seconds. Now open your mouth so I can pour a gallon of hand sanitizer on your tongue.

8. "Agggghhhhh, my ears, my ears! Someone's stabbing my eardrums out with a screwdriver!" Yup, as the plane goes up or down, this is what my kids are screaming as the pressure pops their ears. Coincidentally it's the same thing the people in front of us are yelling because my kids won't shut up. What's that you say? Give them gum? Oh that's a GREAT idea, three years from now when they're older and I know they won't spit it out in my hair and then purposely rub it all around.

9. Can the airplane lavatory get any smaller? Or stinkier? The answer is yes and yes. If you don't have kids, maybe you haven't noticed that there is a changing table in the airplane bathroom. Yes, in that two-foot space. Or rather a flat plastic shelf that pulls down over the scary ass toilet. You know how hard it is

using the lavatory when there's turbulence? Now try doing that with a screaming, wriggly toddler on a plastic shelf.

The only good news is the lavatory is so small even if you hit a big bump there's no room for either of you to go anywhere. The bad news is the bathroom was just contaminated by an old lady who spent 14 minutes in there (so long you almost told the flight attendant in case she died. Alas, she didn't die but it smells like something did), and your kid's poopie diaper manages to make it smell even worse. I know some people choose to forgo the lav and change the baby's diaper in the seat itself, but you know what happens then? I mean besides everyone who already hates you stabbing you with their eye daggers even more. The baby pees mid diaper change and 27D is suddenly 27PP and you have to sit in urine for the rest of the flight because every other seat is booked.

10. Dear people who sat in our row after us, I'm sorry. I'm sorry for the goldfish all shoved in between the seats where the airplane cleaners couldn't get them. I'm sorry for the funky smell of my kid's vomit that will probably linger for weeks. I'm sorry for the lollipop you may have found on page 46 of the Sky Mall magazine. And most of all I'm sorry you reached into your seat pocket and accidentally grabbed the rest of a mushy, slobbery, spit-covered banana that my kid put in there because he wouldn't eat the brown spot. I meant to hand it to the flight attendant but I have like 9 million things I'm trying to remember when I get off the plane.

Well, that's ten and I'm too lazy to write any more since this is practically a novel already, but God help you if your kid decides to flush the airplane toilet while she's sitting on it. And God help you if your flight is delayed especially while you're on the tarmac and they turn off the AC to conserve energy. And God help you if they lose your luggage and Binky the F'ing cuddle bear is packed in that suitcase. And God help you if your kid drinks the whole can of apple juice and it gives her the runs on the airplane seat. So basically just hope to God that God helps you because flying with rug rats is pretty much hell on earth. Or rather hell 10,000 feet above earth.

Minivan for the week: $650
One tank of gas: $60
Three tickets to Disney World: $277
Seeing my daughter's face on the Teacups: priceless

You know those pregnancy tests that show a smiley face if you're preggers? Do they have ones that show a frowny face for teenagers? Or for moms who already have kids and know what the F it's like?

Don't Read This Chapter While You are Eating Chocolate

ME: Zoey, why didn't you go to the potty? Why did you poop in your Pull-Up?

ZOEY: Well, I tooted and then I pushed and pushed and pushed and it just came out.

ME: Thanks Zoey. I'm so glad I know how a poop works now.

THIS ONE DOESN'T HAVE ANY PICTURES. YOU'RE WELCOME.

You know the feeling. You're standing in the middle of Gymboree walking around a parachute singing the Farmer in the Dell and wondering three things:

1.   WTF is a dell?
2.   Is this seriously what my life has come to?
3.   Why does my kid have that weird look on his face?

Oh shit. Literally. You can read the signs from a mile away. The watery eyes, the vein popping out of his forehead, the look of determination. Yup, he's pooping. OMG, kid, didn't I just change your dipe dipe like thirty seconds ago? How many times can you poop in a day? And then about ten minutes later when Chippy McChipper is singing Gymbo the clown waves bye bye bye, your kid is finally done. Wait, nope, a little more. And now he's done. Hopefully.

So it's off to the public restroom you go with your adorable Petunia Picklebottom diaper bag only there's really nothing adorable about this scenario. Because let's face it, changing poopie diapers sucks ass.

From the moment they're born to the moment they finally drop their first log in the potty (Mommmmm, wiiiiipe meeeee!), you'll change over 3,000 poopie diapers. No, I didn't say diapers. I said POOPIE diapers.

And yes, I did the math. Unless you have one of those weird kids who only poops like once every four days, in which case I hate you and please stop reading this now because I refuse to entertain people like you.

So here goes. Ten poopie diaper scenarios that make me wish my kids were born without tushes. Awww shit, you know some jackass reading this is all pissed off now because some kids *are* born without tushes, and I'm an a-hole for making fun of them. Well, I apologize in advance to anyone whose kid doesn't have a tush. Wait, no I don't. I'll trade ya.

1.   Remember when your kid was a newborn and they pooped like a million times a day and you thought it was disgusting only it wasn't really because they weren't even eating solids yet and you had no idea what was coming in a few months? But then once in a while something truly disgusting *would* happen. You'd have them on the changing table and you'd undo their diaper and suddenly they'd start pooping right then and there. And:

    A. Either it's projectile poop and travels whatever the distance is to the nearest wall. Yes, even if you're outside and the nearest wall is 200 feet away.

    Or B. It's regular poop and you have to stand there watching it ooze out of them like one of those frigging Play-Doh machines that you push down the lever and make the Play-Doh come out of a hole (a hole not a-hole). And you kind of have to keep watching because you need to know when he's finished only it feels really wrong to watch poop come out of your kid's tush. Like really really wrong.

2.   Ho-hummm, I wonder what I can do to make my mommy's job harder. Oh, I know! I'm gonna dip my feet into the pupu platter and watch her freak out and say, "Nooooo," and then wipe them down with a wipe like a thousand times. And then just as soon as she's done I'm gonna stick my feet in my mouth and really freak her out.

3.   Okay, if there's one thing I've learned from Grey's Anatomy it's that all doctors are hot and like to have sex in the on-call room. And if there are two things I've learned it's how to scrub each finger individually with lots of soap. So why the hell when I change a poopie diaper and I scrub like that do my fingers still smell like poop for the rest of the day? Because if they still smell, I have to assume it's because they have poo particles on them, which is just awesome when you're eating French fries later and your friends are like, "That's weird, why do you eat fries with a fork?" "Umm, because my fingers are speckled with poo particles."

4.   Okay, where is the cameraman? Surely someone is going to pop out at any moment and shout, "You've been punk'd" or, "You're on Candid Camera" or some shit like that because there is no way this ginormous crap the size of Rhode Island came out of this tiny little baby. Surely they did a Folgers coffee switch and had a man poop in a diaper and put it on my little one when I wasn't looking.

5.   What smells? Well, I know it's not my kid because I just changed his diaper like three minutes ago. And so begins the poop-smelling domino effect around Gymboree. One mom after another yanks her kid towards her by the waistband and

fearlessly buries her nose in his tush. After a few minutes, I finally do the same. Whew-eeee! Did you seriously do that again?! Only when I take a peek inside there's nothing. Ahhhh, the residual poop smell on the pants. Rogue poop particles again. Is it wrong to spray your kid's butt with Febreze?

6. Whatta you mean they don't make size ten diapers? Yeah, his tush fits in a four, but his poop doesn't. Hence the giant brown amoeba moving up his back. So basically I have two choices. Either he gets a shampoop when I take his onesie off over his head, or I'm breaking out the scissors and cutting off his onesie which is now more of a number twosie. When is someone going to invent a diaper turtleneck that'll protect the entire back? Or a full diaper scuba outfit? Million. Dollar. Idea.

7. Have you ever wrestled a greased pig? No, me neither. But I could. I could seriously win like the redneck Olympics of greased pig wrestling because that's what I do every damn day. At some age babies start to HATE being on the changing table, and the second you get the diaper off they're basically a rolling pin on a pile of poop. Yo Darwin, I used to believe your theories but now I'm starting to think you're wrong. 'Cause if evolution were really happening, moms would have eight arms. At least. And noses that couldn't smell. And larger vajayjays. Not that that has anything to do with changing poopie diapers. Just sayin'.

8. Oh hello blueberries and black beans and corn. Fancy meeting you here. Not. So basically what you're telling me is that the twenty minutes I spent making my kid's food dance and sing and vroom vroom like an F'ing truck was a total waste of time and that my kid's getting zero nutrition. Awesome.

9.   So I'm about to change a poopie diaper and I think I have it all under control when I reach into the wipes and oh shit. There's only one wipe left. Agggh, I'm gonna kill my husband (even though I have no idea if he was the last one to use the wipes, but I can't help from being mad at him still). Anyways, I have to somehow manage to clean alllll of this poo with one measly little wipe. So I wind up folding it like 96 times, and by the end I'm basically wiping the poo with my fingertips. Hellllo, poo particle French fries.

10. (Please sing the following to the tune of "Smelly Cat" from *Friends*)

Sticky poo, sticky poo,
Did my kid eat Elmer's glue?
Sticky poo, sticky poo,
Go the F away.

I've already used 9,000 wipes,
It shouldn't take this long to change a dipe,
I feel like Lady MacBeth here,
When I'm done I'll surely need a beer.

Sticky Poo, sticky poo,
I need a Brillo pad,
Sticky poo, sticky poo,
You suck my assssss.

Alrighty then, ass seems like the perfect word to end this on.

Tents are F'ing AWESOME! Until one kid poops and it's like a Dutch oven that singes all of your nose hairs.

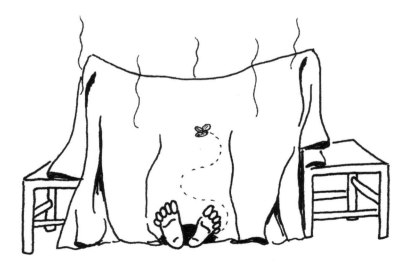

POOP MOBILE

You know when Dateline goes into a hotel room and shines that black light thingie all over everything to show where all the fecal matter is and the remote control is like an F'ing hot zone? I mean it looks like someone needed to go to the bathroom but the housekeeper was cleaning it or something so they just crouched down and laid a log right on the remote control. Someone once told me to bring a Ziploc bag on vacation because you can still work the remote through the bag. Well, lemme ask you this. Would you hold someone else's poop log in a plastic bag? Hells no. I'll just walk up to the TV from now on if I need to change the channel. In my Hazmat suit.

Anyways, would you believe that this post is actually about the library? I shit you not. Pun totally intended.

The way I feel when I enter a library is pretty much the way I feel when I hear from Dateline that the remote is covered in fecal matter. Because A. You can't clean paper, so books like NEVER get cleaned. B. There's always that weird, unsettling smell when you open a library book. And C. What do people do when they're taking a shit? They read. Library books. While they're pooping. Before they wash their hands. If I were younger I would put an emoticon here with someone throwing up, but alas the only emoticons forty-year-olds know are smiley face and frowny face. So ☹.

Anyways, I kind of think my toddler likes to feed my fear because guess what that little a-hole (and I'm speaking literally) does every time we're there. He takes a great big, giant poop. And to make things worse, guess what I do every time. I forget the diaper bag in the car. Every F'ing time.

Like today. There we are in the library reading Winnie the Pooh (not really, but it makes this story better and I can't remember what the F we were reading anyway because really I just read the words while I think about something else like chocolate or wine), when he sneaks behind the couch so he can be all stealthy and shit. Yeahhh, real F'ing stealthy kiddo. A. I see your forehead with that massive purple vein all bulging out which only happens when you're pushing out a poop or when you're having an aneurism (hells yeah, I spelled it right on the first try!). And B. The whole library can hear you grunting.

Of course it's at this moment that I realize I left the diaper bag in the car. Are you kidding me? The way I see it I have two options:

Option 1: I can look around for some non-pedophiley person in the library to watch him while I dash to the car as fast as humanly possible to grab the diaper bag. So I look around the library. Pedophile, porn surfer, pedophile, homeless person, nanny who's paying more attention to her phone than the kid she's supposedly watching, guy with a monocle in the reference section, porn surfer, pedophile. Shit, does nobody normal go to the library?

Option 2: I can make him leave early and do the dreaded diaper change on the floor of the car. Little did I know leaving him with Mr. Peanut in the reference section would have been less frightening.

Moms, you know that one poop a month that makes you wish you were born with three arms? This was one of those. Out the sides, up the back, coming out of places I didn't even know existed. Does my son have some kind of second tush somewhere I don't know about? Surely the doctor would have noticed that when he was born, but I have to wonder. Seriously, how can so much poop come from this tiny little being? It takes every bit of skill I have to keep poop from getting on the car carpet.

Well, fifteen minutes later, I manage to survive and so does the car. Barely. And the air is like seriously contaminated. I drive home in thirty-degree weather with all four windows rolled down and my head sticking out the window like a dog so I can breathe, my jowls flapping in the wind. And I swear to God the next time we go to the library I won't forget the diaper bag. Of course, that's what I said the last time.

ZOEY: *Somebody has to come and wipe me because I pooped a BIG one.*

This sentence basically sums up my job description. I think I'm going to add it to my Linked In profile.

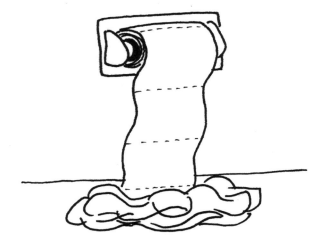

JUST A RANDOM POOP STORY THAT HAS NOTHING TO DO WITH MY RUG RATS

Once I worked at Express in the 90's (what's even more cliché is that I rollerbladed there), and every day around lunchtime someone would go into the Gap next door and take a dump in their dressing room. WTF, right? I'd love to know what was going through this guy's mind when he did it the first time. Was he like, "I'm crazy and I think it'd be fun to take a crap in here?" Or was he like, "Shit, I have six more outfits to try on but I really have to go to the bathroom?" Probably a bit of both.

Anyways, the first time it happened the employees were all like, "Ewww gross." The second time they were like, "WTF?" And the third time they were like, "Oh no you di'n't."

So one day there was a big stakeout to figure out who was the shitter. I wasn't there to see it since I worked next door (thank F'ing God) but I can just picture all of the employees leaning over in the dressing room to see under the doors. Feet, feet, feet, feet, feet with a bare ass. Annnd, mystery solved. Although I always wonder whether they stopped him before he pooped that day or whether they needed to catch him in the act. And then did they let him finish or did they make him pinch the loaf mid poop? Yes, I'm a little F'ed in the head, but thanks to this experience, I know there's at least one person who's more F'ed up than I am.

HELLS YEAH I'M PUTTING ON MY OXYGEN MASK BEFORE MY KID'S

Awww shit, my nose is broken. Nahh, not like some douchebag kicked it in and broke it. Like the smell function has gone kaput. Yup, I found this out on the way to Florida. Hells yeah, Florida, where the sun always shines and people eat in restaurants as early as we do.

Anyways, we get through TSA, which I'm convinced stands for Totally Sucks Ass, and now we're sitting on the airplane flying at 30,000 feet. My younger son, Holden, has apparently taken some NoDoz when I wasn't looking because he's bouncing off the plastic walls, and Zoey is comatose in front of the iPad watching Caillou, which amazingly still annoys me even though she's wearing earphones and I can't hear his whiny ass voice.

I hear the people behind us talking about something that smells bad and I realize that Holden has just pooped his brains out, which wouldn't be a big deal except the seatbelt sign is illuminated so we have no choice but to change him on the tray table. Awesome. Don't worry, we scrubbed it down with hand sanitizer afterwards. Not really, but let's just pretend we did. Besides, I'm sure the airlines clean them really well between flights. Bwahahahaha!

Anyways, towards the middle of the flight I get a whiff of the poopie smell again. Are you F'ing kidding me? Again?! I swear kids save their shit up for days so they can do it like a thousand times while you're traveling. Luckily this time we can use the lavatory so Greg offers to change him, which sounds like he's trying to be nice but really he just can't take Caillou anymore.

While they're gone I can hear the people talking behind me again. Apparently one of them is actually getting sick over the smell. Hmm, I don't really smell anything, but when Greg gets back I'll ask him to take Zoey next just in case.

"No poop!" Greg reports back to me as he hands me Holden and picks up Zoey to take her.

Ohhh shit. As soon as he picks her up, I see it and get a giant whiff. There it is, straight out of a Stephen King movie, a giant brown amoeba oozing up the back of her pants. And the smell is atrocious. Why the hell didn't those oxygen masks drop from the ceiling?

So here's the bad part. Can you F'ing believe it? I haven't even gotten to the bad part yet. The seat she's been sitting in is made out a dark pattern to disguise stains, but I lean over to smell and examine it more closely and there it is. A giant diarrhea spot on more than half of the seat cushion. Who the hell knew your seat cushion can be used as a floater device too?

OMG, what the hell do I do? Should I ring the call button? I can't decide so I casually cover the wet spot with a burp cloth and wait for Greg to get back with our daughter, the Grand Poobah. When he does I tell him what's going on, and he says, "Go figure," and kindly hands me a baggie with her spontaneously-combustible pants inside. "We have to tell the flight attendant," I say, thinking about the person who has to sit in this seat on the next flight. "What if they charge us for the cleaning?" he worries. Can you imagine? $35 for extra leg room. $100 for a poopie seat. Man, these airlines will milk you for anything.

Still, I'm not a total a-hole so I can't *not* say something (if my high school English teacher is reading this, she's totally cringing at that double negative. Take that, Mrs. Meany Pants). So on the way out I whisper to the flight attendant, "You might want to check seat 27F. I think my daughter's diaper leaked a little." So the flight attendant is like, "Sure, buh-bye," and clearly ignoring me. "No, I'm fucking serious," I say. Well, I didn't actually say the word fucking with my mouth, but I said it with my eyes and now she can tell I mean business. "Oh, okay, we definitely will."

But I gotta wonder. Why didn't I smell the poop for so long? I mean the guy behind me was literally getting sick over it. Is it possible I've officially changed too many diapers and my nose is broken? Or is it like a Brita pitcher and I need to change the filter or something? I'll have to go to Bed, Bath and Beyond to see if they carry nose filters. What section would they be in? Definitely not Bed. Bath or Beyond? Woo-hooo, I just remembered I have a 20% off coupon!

Yeah, I fully expect to be senile and smearing poop all over the walls one day. I just hope I'm living with one of my kids when it happens. Payback's a bitch.

ITTY-BITTY POTTY PARTY

Once when Zoey was little I took her to the bathroom at the zoo, and when we were next in line one of the stalls opened up to reveal an itty-bitty potty just for little girls like her. I swear the angels sang in the heavens when she saw it. She had the most wonderful potty experience ever. Then it was my turn.

ME: Okay, let's go find Mommy a potty.

ZOEY: No Mommy, use this one.

While I really wanted to find a normal potty for myself, two things went through my head:

1. You know how that first person in line right now is all filled with anticipation because she's next? I'd have to go out there and burst her bubble and tell her why I'm allowed to cut in front of her because I already waited in line and now I need a different stall with a normal-sized potty.

2. Zoey's always using my big potties. It can't hurt to use her little one just this once.

What the hell, why not? So I dropped my pants and crouched down to go. Way down. Wayyyy down. I'm not exaggerating. This is how low this potty was. You know how you can see people's feet beneath the stalls? Nikes, Pumas, Crocs, someone's big ass, Adidas, Keds. I wish I were kidding.

Dear anyone who saw my ass that day,
I'm sorry you saw what you saw.
I'm sorry if I caused you to go blind.
I'm sorry if I scarred you for life.
Sincerely,
Baby Sideburns' got a big ole butt, oh yeah

FIVE BROWN SHIT DOTS

Okay, the other night I'm out for drinks with a friend when she tells me something that's been going on in her house and I'm like, "Nooo," and she's like, "Yes," and I'm like, "Noooooo," and she's like, "Yessssss, I couldn't make this up if I tried." This is her story (retold by me because she didn't make it funny enough and didn't use enough curse words):

So last week she was going to the bathroom and enjoying her People magazine, la la la la laaaa. She had two pages left to read in an article and unless it sounded like her kids were playing with guns or building WMDs outside the bathroom door, she wasn't getting up for anything.

Kabooooom! Awwww shit, of course the second she thought it they did it. WTF was that? Someone's head? A Molotov cocktail? The cat in the microwave? Fine, she said, and started to get up. Which totally sucked because now she couldn't finish her People magazine article and she'd have no idea WTF happened at Jessica Simpson's baby shower. How ever would she go on living?

So she reached to get some toilet paper and whoaaa, WTF is that? No seriously, WTF WTF WTF? You're not going to believe what she found. There they were sitting right there in the middle of the clean white toilet paper. Five haphazardly-placed shit dots. Holy. Crap. Five brown shit dots.

FRIEND: Woody!!!!!!!! Get in here!

WOODY: Hi.

FRIEND: What is this?

WOODY: Toilet paper.

Duh.

FRIEND: No, what's ON the toilet paper?

WOODY: I had to check.

FRIEND: Check what?

WOODY: To make sure I'm clean.

FRIEND: Uhhh, you're not.

Anyways, in case it isn't obvious, her four-year-old had been learning how to wipe himself, you know, back there. But how the hell do you teach a kid how to wipe enough? It never occurred to my friend that she would have to explain these things in intricate detail, but they're kids. How else are they supposed to learn? "You take some toilet paper and you wipe and then you fold it and find a clean section and you wipe again, and you repeat this until the TP comes back clean or until you run out of room and you need to rip off some more toilet paper."

So since my friend didn't tell her son EXACTLY what to do in explicit detail, he came up with his own method. You wipe and then you use your finger like a dipstick in your tush to see if it comes back clean.

Only it never comes back clean because you're not even four and can't wipe worth shit.

See, kids have no clue unless we tell them these things. Like here's a story about my other friend's kid. So one day his mom walked into the living room and he was having total itchy butt and was dragging his ass on the carpet like a dog with worms, so she asked him what was wrong. Apparently he had stopped wiping.

JASMINE: (with alarm) Why aren't you wiping?

ITCHY BUTT: I didn't know how many squares of toilet paper to use.

WHAT???!!! This cracks me up for all sorts of reasons. Knowing my friend, she was all nice to him and casually took her kid into the bathroom to show him how many squares to use, but if this were my child, here's what I would have said.

ME: Okay, kid, I get it. This stuff can be confusing. But are you kidding me? Zero squares? ZERO?! Ennhhh, wrong! I think we all know ZERO is NOT the correct answer. Like if this were on a multiple-choice test:

How many squares of toilet paper do you use when you take a dump?

A.   One
B.   Three
C.   Five
D.   More

See? Zero isn't even an option.

My point is this. Whoever says potty training can happen in three days is lying their ass off. Potty training takes YEARS. Sure, they might be peeing in the potty right away. But some of them won't poop in there. Some of them won't do it at night. Some of them won't go on a public potty. Some of them create beautiful Jackson Pollock-like urine paintings on the walls. Some of them don't know how many squares to use. And some of them wipe brown shit dots on the toilet paper for their mom to find. Awesome.

ANOTHER HOLIDAY?
ARE YOU F'ING KIDDING
ME?

NEW YEARS RESOLUTIONS I PLAN ON BREAKING THE SHIT OUT OF

Ordinarily when I catch a glimpse of my naked self in the mirror I have a few reactions:

1. I throw up in my mouth a little but then swallow it (you'd think after seeing my naked body I'd fully throw up to expel a few calories)
2. I look around for a black Sharpie to mark up my body so I can fantasize that I have an appointment with Dr. 90210
3. I want to eat my muffin top

But for the past 40 days (between Thanksgiving and New Years) I've had a completely different reaction. Who gives a shit how I look right now because come New Years Day, I'm going on a health kick. And come to think of it, it's not just about eating. By February I plan on looking like a tall skinny blonde who's hairless from the nose down, minus the tall and blonde part. Plus like a million other things I want to change too. So here goes. Twelve New Years resolutions I plan on breaking the shit out of:

1. I will no longer eat my kids' leftover French fries, chicken nuggets, bagels, sandwich crusts, ice cream cones, cake frosting, pizza crusts, etc. etc. etc. Because last year I was basically a human food disposal. I might as well have just

tipped my head backwards over the sink and let people scrape their plates straight into my mouth. It would have been less degrading than the way I cram ten French fries into my mouth as we're packing up to leave a restaurant. And then ten more while I'm pretending to double-check the table for anything we forgot. I fail to notice that we're leaving behind my kid's favorite sippy cup, but oh shit, look what we did forget. Ten greasy ass French fries.

2.   One night a month I will try to wear a sexy nightgown to bed. I mean without putting on fat pants and a disgusting long-sleeved t-shirt over it, even if it means shivering all night long and having to warm my hands between the blubber of my thighs.

3.   Speaking of blubber, from now on when I undress at the end of the day and my husband drools and says, "Yeah yeah yeah," I won't roll my eyes and look at him like he must be insane.

4.   I will no longer turn into Glenn Close from Fatal Attraction when my daughter won't put on her shoes. Zoey, put on your shoes. Zoey, put on your shoes. Zoey, put on your shoes. ZOEY, PUT ON YOUR FUCKING SHOES RIGHT FUCKING NOW OR I'M GOING TO RIP YOUR FUCKING HEAD OFF AND LEAVE YOU AT HOME WHILE WE GO TO DISNEY WORLD WITHOUT YOU!!!!!! Just so it's clear I didn't actually say the word "fucking" to my kiddo. I just wrote it in there to illustrate how much I was yelling. In real life I speak with giant pauses while I think the curse words in my head.

5.   I will stop throwing giant fistfuls of Cheerios out of my kid's car seat into parking lots. I know they're biodegradable but

before it rains some poor schmuck is probably going to step on them first and that's just annoying. Believe me I know. I step on Cheerios every goddamn day of my life so I'm like an expert at it.

6. I will finally unsubscribe from Pottery Barn, Toys R Us and Michaels emails, but I will try not to feel like a loser if my inbox is empty when I wake up in the morning. Why in God's name it makes me feel popular that World Market emails me at three in the morning is beyond me.

7. I will check my magnification mirror daily to make sure I notice my one-haired goatee BEFORE someone else does.

8. There are 1095 meals in a year (not including midnight snacks, brunches, and drunken moments when I shovel handfuls of bacon bits into my mouth). I promise to stay seated for the duration of one of those 1095 meals. Just one.

9. I will not forget one key item every time I go grocery shopping. Do not forget the buns. Do not forget the buns. Do not forget the buns. And then I'm standing in the parking lot loading the bags into the car and guess what I F'ing forgot. The buns. But the kids are already loaded in and I would have to unload them and reload them which is worse than being water-boarded, so I guess we're having sloppy joes without the buns. The unintentional Atkins diet.

10. I will remember that the three-second rule cannot be lengthened to thirty seconds or thirty days, even when the Oreo I find under the table is fuzz-free.

11. I have heard that if you spend less than $50 at Target they don't make you sign for it. It's one of those suburban myths. I will go to Tarjay and attempt to spend less than $50 to see if it's true. Attempt.

12. I will no longer lick my finger and clean my kid's face. Replacing the chocolate with saliva does not make it clean even if you can't see the saliva.

Dear Uterus,

I just want to say thank you soooo much for the very thoughtful Valentine's Day gift today. Now I can totally pretend like I planned on "doing it" tonight.

XOXOXO

Love,
Your BFF

TEN THINGS THAT SUCK ABOUT VALENTINE'S DAY

(easiest list I've ever come up with)

Awwww shit, it's that holiday again. All in favor of adding February 29th to the calendar and taking February 14th away, say aye! Because seriously, do we seriously need a frigging holiday to tell us to express our love?

As far as I'm concerned, I tell my kiddo I love him every time I change his disgusting poopie diaper. Would I be up to my elbows in his green dinarena if I didn't love him? I think not. And do you see this chair that looks like a giant piece of dookie?

Would I let my husband keep this in our house if I didn't love him? (side note, by the time of publication the chair was gone) And well, the fact that I don't kill our 4-year-old every day is the biggest token of my affection you can get.

So here's the thing. It's not just me. I'm willing to bet that Valentine's Day sucks for more than 50% of the population. No, I didn't do a scientific study, but I'm making an educated guess. Based on what? Based on this shit. Here are the top ten things that suck about V-Day:

1. This holiday literally makes bad couples stay together. Like when I was young and dating I distinctly remember not breaking up with someone because Valentine's Day was in like 8 days. Awww shit, I can't dump his ass now. It's almost V-Day and that'd just be mean. Plus, then I'd be alone on V-Day. And of course, then he bought me an expensive piece of jewelry that I had to accept because he didn't know I was going to dump him later that week, which I couldn't do now because he bought me an expensive piece of jewelry.

2. This holiday also does the complete opposite and makes people break up because the pressure is just too much. Like once I made this jackass cookies for V-Day and he gave me the whole "I don't think we should be *that* serious" speech. WTF? Is it because I made them heart-shaped? Cupid's like the only other F'ing shape there is for this stupid holiday, so you'd rather me give you a naked baby? What kind of message does that send?

3. Dear Parents, please have your kids sign their name on 17 cards and bring them into school this Friday. And please plan on staying at school for a few minutes to help your kids put

them in the mailboxes. And please no candy. So here's what I have to say about that. A. V-Day cards are like the size of a post-it note, so getting my 4-year-old to write her name that small once, much less 17 times, is like crazy impossible. B. I take three showers a week. So when you make ME sign and stuff 17 cards because my kid was more interested in playing with a box of tampons, basically you're taking away one of my showers. Which isn't good for anyone. C. Does this mean my kid is bringing home 17 cards? They better be recyclable because F that shit coming into my house. D. No candy?! Then WTF am I supposed to steal from my kid?

4. Guess who else hates Valentine's Day. Van Damme, Vin Diesel and The Rock. Guess who else. Every other guy on this planet. Because I'll tell you what movie isn't being watched on February 14th. Anything with even a hint of an explosion. But guess what is being watched. That movie where Meryl Streep joins a book club where they all look at their vajayjays in handheld mirrors until she bumps into some Italian schmuck and they fall in love and make love under a covered bridge in Madison County. Yes, I made that shit up, but aren't all chick flicks basically that?

5. Ohhhh honey, let's eat at that restaurant we love for Valentine's Day. I'll make reservations. HOSTESS: Two for dinner? Lovely. We have openings at 4pm or 11pm but we don't actually open until 5 and you have to leave by 11:15. So you end up at F'ing Chilis sharing an oh-so-romantic awesome blossom. Awesome.

6. You know all that shit they sell for V-Day presents like boxers and socks and t-shirts with hearts all over them? There's no better way to waste your money. Because there is only one day

a year you can wear that shit. On Valentine's Day. You can't even wear it the week leading up to V-Day because you know you want to wear it on V-Day itself and that festive shit is so obvious everyone will notice you wore the same thing twice in one week and they'll think that's gross even if you washed it. Unless you wear a sign that says *I washed it,* but that's just weird.

7.   Red, pink and purple do not go together. They F'ing clash. But for some reason everyone pretends like they do on V-Day. Even though they DON'T.

8.   As if V-Day didn't suck enough when you were single, it's practically worse when you're married because you're all like, seriously, I just paid like 9 million dollars for Christmas presents and now I have to buy more presents? So you and your spouse agree that you're not going to spend more than $20, which actually sucks even worse because do you know how hard it is to find something romantic for $20. This is the reason I have a closet downstairs filled with shit like a Slanket and a lap desk.

9.   Great, another holiday that's all about eating crap. I know people are all like whatevs, it's only one F'ing day a year, but it's not one F'ing day. Because every day it's some holiday or some birthday or a holiday because it's someone's birthday (ahem, Jesus) or a birthday party with cake to celebrate a birthday that's four days later when there will also be cake to eat on the actual birthday. And V-Day might be the worst because A. Most of it is chocolate which is irresistible and a sin to throw away. And B. I have to bite like every piece until I find the one

that's filled with caramel and I even eat that nasty one with the gross pink stuff inside.

10. I remember when my hubby and I started dating and we'd write like a whole novel in our thoughtfully picked out V-Day cards. Like we had to write on both sides of the card and even the back sometimes and draw an arrow to tell you to turn the card over. Duh, in case you didn't realize "I love the way you" wasn't the end of the sentence. And then as we dated longer, it shrank into a shorter paragraph. And then by the time we were married, it was like "I love you, xoxoxox, Love, me." And now that we have kids we just buy the first card we pick up in the store and scribble "Love, me" on it. I'm pretty much thinking that by the time we're 80 we're just going to sign our cards with a single dot.

Roses are red,
Violets are blue,
To the grandparents who all sent musical cards to the kids,
F.U.

DAYLIGHT SAVINGS
CAN KISS MY ASS

Seriously? Are you kidding me? My kids are finally both sleeping through the night so of course it's time to F with their schedule. Time to change the stupid clocks AGAIN. Here's what I think about Daylight Savings Time:

1. At first I have to run it through my head— Spring forward, Fall back—so this time we set the clocks forward. Wait, is that a good thing? And then I remember it's never a good thing anymore. It was good when I was single and partying and we got an extra hour of sleep in the Fall, but now I'm a parent and they both SUCK ASS.

2. Yeah, I know it's going to seem awesome tomorrow morning when I look at the clock and it's 7AM and neither kid is up yet, but it's total bullshit. Because tomorrow night when I'm trying to put the kids down for bed at 7:30, it's really only 6:30, and it's gonna be like they downed 6 Red Bulls and three 5-Hour Energies right before getting tucked in. Does anyone know where I can buy some of those restraining straps they have at mental hospitals because I'm going to need some to keep them in bed?

3.   I love walking through the house the next day and trying to figure out which appliance is modern enough to change on its own and which ones I need to change manually. And by love I mean hate.

4.   And of all the ones I have to change manually, when I hold the button down does it scroll through the numbers quickly or does it tick... by... one... at... a... time... until... you.... want... to... kill...yourself? So finally you just start pressing the button over and over again really fast and want to kill yourself again when you accidentally go past the number you meant to stop at.

5.   And then you're playing downstairs with the kids in the playroom a few days later and there are twenty minutes until naptime, until suddenly you realize the clock you've been looking at was never changed. Aggggh! It's like 40 minutes PAST naptime! Which explains why your kids are such cranky a-holes and why they'll be cranky later today too when you have to wake them up so they don't sleep too late and ruin their bedtime.

6.   Maybe I'm an idiot, but why is it so crazy hard to change the clock in the car? (yeah, that makes sense, turn OFF the power to change it. WTF???) So for weeks you don't change it and every time you look at it you just add an hour in your head. And then one day you get to school a little early and you use the time you're waiting to finally change the clock, only every time you look at the clock from now on you keep adding an hour to it because now it's a habit. So A. You think you're always running late. And B. You're totally wasting valuable

brainpower (hysterical that I spelled brainpower wrong the first time) by doing unnecessary math.

7. I've heard that Daylight Savings still exists for the farmers. Now I'm all for farmers, but F that. I mean how many farmers are in this country? Now how many parents are there? We win.

ME: Want to dye Easter eggs today?
ZOEY: Yeah!!! (pause) But why do the eggs have to be killed?
And why was she so excited to kill something??

TEN THINGS I REALLY F'ING WANT FOR MOTHER'S DAY

1.   I don't want to wipe a single ass all day. I think all kids should have to hold in their poop in on Mother's Day. Now that would make it special.

2.   I want brunch. But not with the whole frigging family. I want brunch with my other mommy friends. See ya, rug rats. Mommy's coming back drunk on laughter and bloody marys.

3.   I want to sleep in. But not with my hooligans shouting "MOMMYYYYYY!!!" at the top of their lungs and ramming one of those giant cannon thingies into the door to bust inside. To all the hubbies reading this: when the rugrats wake up, take them outside immediately. Not downstairs. OUTSIDE. That's right, scoop them up in a football hold and rush them out the door. I'm F'ing serious. Change their diapers and their clothes on the front lawn if you have to. Just don't let them wake my ass up.

4.   I want a card. But not a stupid Hallmark card. I want one of those awesome homemade ones made with macaroni. Only I want the macaroni cooked and poured into a bowl and covered with a delicious cream sauce and paired with a giant bottle of red wine.

5. Jewelry jewelry jewelry. Unless it's one of those stupid necklaces made with cheap plastic beads. None of that shit. Unless Tiffany's is suddenly selling overpriced plastic bead necklaces. That can be returned for money. Because I don't want to exchange it and the only thing I can afford is a stupid ass pen or a keychain.

6. I want you to cook breakfast for me. In someone else's kitchen.

7. I want to pee and poop alone. I will prepare for the day by downing a tanker truck full of liquid and eating ridiculous amounts of fiber.

8. I want chocolate. But not just any ole chocolate. I want the kind that someone has taken a fat Sharpie to and blacked out the F'ing calorie section.

9. I want a good present. Like one I'll really like. It's not the thought that counts. It's MY thought that counts. And my thought should not be WTF?

10. I want ten "Leave me the fuck alone" coupons with no expiration date.

TWAS THE NIGHT BEFORE MOTHER'S DAY

Twas the night before Mother's Day and all through the house,
Not a creature was stirring, not even the fish (because he might be
dead, not sure unless I jiggle the tank),
The coats were all slung on the floor without care,
Hoping someone else would pick them up there.

The Mommy was nestled all snug in her bed,
While visions from pinot danced through her head.
All dressed in my nightgown with fat pants on too,
Just dreaming tomorrow I could sit alone and poo.

When outside my room there arose such a clatter,
I sprang from my bed to see what was the matter,
Someone's lamp? A book? Did someone fall out of bed?
No, none of these things, something else instead.

I ran to the hallway, threw open the door,
And what did I find? A hole straight through the floor,
A bowling ball is great when it's where it's meant to be,
But through my hardwood floors, are you F'ing kidding me?

TEN THINGS DAD REALLY F'ING

WANTS FOR FATHER'S DAY

Okay, so I really hoped Mr. Baby Sideburns would write something for Father's Day, but that F'er is so lazy he never got around to it. And by lazy I mean going to work every day so he can put food on the table that my kids won't eat. And coming home every night to put the kids in the bathtub and shit like that because I'll tear my hair out and cut my ears off if I have to spend another second with my little love muffins.

Anyways, what I'm trying to say is that he's an awesomely amazing father and while I'm probably not going to give him any of the following because I got him this totally kickass keychain that says "I am Fartacus," if I asked him what he really wants for Father's Day, this is what I imagine he would say:

1.   I want an hour on the toilet. I know you think my man chair is that ugly recliner in the living room that looks like a piece of doodie (your words not mine), but it is not. The toilet is my throne. And I want to sit there uninterrupted until I've got ring-around-the-tush, until a hemroid (spelled the way it should be) is popping out, and until I've made a turd that's big enough and worthy enough to take a picture of with my phone so I can send it to my friends.

2.   I don't know where you made reservations that day, but I want to be able to wear what I want to wear there (take that Dr.

Seuss). I'm not going to be a total slob, but I don't want to be told not to wear jeans and then we get to the restaurant and there are all these guys wearing jeans.

3.   I don't want to hear the words "I want Mommy" that day. Unless someone has a giant poopie diaper or needs to be wiped. Then it's okay.

4.   I want to leave the house to go somewhere and NOT be told to drive safely. I promise I drive safely all the time whether you remind me to or not, but for some reason you think that if you don't tell me this that I'm driving down the road chugging a Colt 45 while I'm blindfolded and holding the steering wheel with my feet.

5.   And speaking of driving, I want to be able to talk about buying a motorcycle one day. Just talk about it. I'm not really gonna buy it, but I would like to be able to have the dream without you telling me my brains will be splattered everywhere, and not because I got in an accident but because you beat the shit out of me for buying a motorcycle.

6.   For once, just once, I would like the kids to play nicely on the floor while I watch a game. I mean I always see this shit on TV—the dad is sitting back all comfy in his man chair with his hand down his pants while the kids are playing with their dolls and trucks on the floor. But that shit never really happens. Really I'm sitting there trying to watch the game while my daughter is jumping up and down in front of the TV set begging me over and over and over again to change the channel to Mother-F'ing-Caillou. Sure I could go watch the game somewhere else,

but then I'm basically a deadbeat father because I've been away from the family at work all week. Or I could record the game and watch it once the hooligans go to bed, but then I can't talk to anyone or answer my phone or look at my texts or read my email or look at Facebook or check twitter all F'ing day because someone's gonna say who won.

7.   WIFE: Which do you like better for the living room, the yellow or the green paint?

ME: The yellow.

WIFE: Okay, we're going with the green.

WIFE: Whatta you think? Cheese dip or guac?

ME: Cheese dip.

WIFE: Hmm, yeah, I'm going to serve guac.

WIFE: Which shoe? Heels or boots?

ME: I like the black ones.

WIFE: They're navy and nahh, I think I like the boots.

Get it? So on Father's Day here's the thing, don't ask for my opinion. Or if you absolutely positively must must must ask me what I think about something, when I give you an answer, go with it. Or at least pretend like you're going with it. Because by the time you actually put the boots on and we're walking out the door, I can't remember which one I picked and I'm not looking at your feet anyways. I'm looking at your boobs.

8. For just one day I don't want to be racked in the balls by my kids. I know they're just playing and they don't mean it, but it hurts like a bitch. Whoever designed children to be exactly the height of my testicles deserves to be punched in the face. A lot. The only good news is that I probably can't have any more kids.

9. I want a blow job. And not the kind that I had to do something to get.

10. Here's a list of the shit I don't want my wife to nag me about on Father's Day: that there's toothpaste on the sink, that I need to shave, that it's garbage day in two days, that I put my shoes in the wrong cubby, that I put my clothes *on* the hamper and not *in* the hamper, that I'm wearing two different black socks (and WTH does that mean anyway, isn't black black?), that I didn't run the garbage disposal, that I forgot to run the dishwasher, that I left streak marks in the toilet (I mean you're lucky I even flushed because I thought about leaving it in there so you could see how amazing it was), that I parked too far to the right, that I parked too far to the left, that I should wear a jacket even if I'm not cold because the kids have to, that I need to make sure when I pump the soap that a little bit doesn't drip out at the end and make a mess (WTF, isn't soap as clean as it gets?), etc. etc. etc.

11. I want a keychain that says "I am Fartacus." Because I am.

Happy take your daughter to work day! Not really, but your husband totally won't know and he'll take her and then you can do awesome things like shower and poop alone all day.

HALLOWEEN IS TO THE JEWS WHAT CHRISTMAS IS TO THE CHRISTIANS

So I'm sure a lot of you are going to be pissed at me for saying this, but being a Jew is not that fun. We kind of got screwed when it comes to pretty much everything. Just about the only things we have that are better are Chinese food and JDate. The rest, not so much.

Let's take Easter for example. On Easter a super adorable bunny hops around and hides eggs full of chocolate and candy for all the little Christian kids to find. Hmmm, what do the Jews have? Well, let's see. Oh, I know! We get to hang fake fruit on the walls of a Sukkah. If you're not Jewish you're probably wondering what the hell is a Sukkah. That's because it's totally lame and instead of chocolate bunnies it involves plastic olives. As if real olives aren't gross enough, someone came along and said let's have a holiday where we decorate a hut with plastic ones.

And then there's Passover. Our firstborns' lives were literally spared and how do we celebrate? By hiding matzo. Seriously? I mean *come on*. Apparently we couldn't come up with something better than searching for flavorless flat bread in the sofa. The least we could do is hide something sweeter like kugel, but probably not in the couch cushions. Over Aunt Ida's dead body.

And then there's the mother of all examples. Christmas verses Hanukkah/Chanukah/Hanukah/Hannukah/Chanuka/Chanukkah.

See, people don't even know how to spell it. Growing up, our Jewish moms always tried to convince us that Hanukkah is even better than Christmas because it lasts eight whole nights as opposed to Christmas that lasts just one. Well, let me ask you this, Moms? Would you rather see one amazing huge fireworks show on July 4th or would you rather it be broken up into lots of dinky shows over eight nights?

So when Christmas rolls around and everyone is decking out their houses in twinkle lights and inflatable Santa Clauses and giant ornaments and candy canes, I myself am green with envy. Have you ever seen the dreidel/menorah section at Michaels? No, you haven't. Because it's about 1/1000th the size of the Christmas section.

So as you can see, I have good reason to feel jealous. Until yesterday. You see yesterday I walked out of my house and my jaw just about hit the ground. We got these new totally awesome Jewish neighbors and guess what they did. They decked out their house in decorations—Halloween decorations! And they went all out. Ghosts and witches and bats and pumpkins and all sorts of awesomeness. So I was envious of her decorations for about thirty seconds. And then one giant trip to Michaels later, my yard was decked out too. Finally the Jews have a holiday we can go to town on!

Yes siree Bob, Halloween can be to the Jews what Christmas is to the Christians. I know what you're thinking, and I'm not talking about all the religiousy Jesus parts of Christmas. Just the superficial fun parts. Although I have a number of friends who will be pissed at me for saying the Jesus stuff isn't fun. You tell me, what's so fun about frankincense and myrrh? I don't even know what those are. They sound about as fun as, hmmmm, I don't know, a sukkah?

Look what Home Depot was selling on clearance! For $25, hells yeah I bought it! Here's what our $25 got us:

1.   *One giant huge amazing light-up Elmo*

2.   *Instant friendship from the neighborhood kids*

3.   *Instant hatred from the neighbors without kids, especially the ones who only put up white lights and those fake candle thingies in every window*

4.   *A giant tantrum from my kids when I try to remove it on January 2nd*

5.   *A letter from our village asking us to remove it because it's April*

WHAT NOT TO F'ING BUY
MY KIDS THIS HOLIDAY

Dear Grammy, Grampy, Nana and Pop Pop,

Ahhh, yes, here we go again. The most wonderful time of the year. For *you*. For me it's more like let's see how much more crap I can fit in my house until TLC comes knocking at my door because they think I'm an F'ing hoarder. I know that you guys are about to jiz (jizz?? giz???) in your pants you're so excited about all the shit you can buy for your grandkids this holiday, but not so fast. Before you whip out your Amex/Target/Mastercards, check out this little list of "guidelines" I've made for you this year. The following is a list of presents *NOT* to buy my kids this holiday.

1.   Anything alive. Because you know what happens to things that are alive? They die. And you know what sucks? Explaining to my kid why Fluffer Nutter the hamster is as hard as a rock and stuck in his tube. And you know what sucks even worse? Fucker Nutter living a healthy life for years and years to come. Because guess who has to clean his E coli-infested poop cage. Yours F'ing truly. As if wiping two asses besides my own isn't enough already.

2.   Stocking stuffers. Or as I like to call them, cheap pieces of shit. I get enough crappy stocking stuffers year-round for free.

They're called McDonald's Happy Meal toys. Would you like fries with that? And how about a plastic piece of crap that was made in China and causes cancer.

3. Any toy that hurts when I accidentally step on it with bare feet. I don't care if the ER doctor is George F'ing Clooney. Getting a bristle block surgically removed from my heel is not worth it.

4. Any toy without an off button. And you know what, I'm going a step further and saying any toy with an off button that doesn't turn off IMMEDIATELY when you push it. You know the crap I'm talking about. You push the off button and it keeps on yapping, "Woof, woof! Thanks for playing! I'll see you again later!" I pushed off. If I wanted you to keep talking I would have pushed the dissertation button. It's like when you're on the phone and you tell someone you have to go and they say okay but then proceed to ask you a thousand questions.

5. Any toy that requires me to play it with them. Toys are how I keep my kids busy while I'm trying to get important things done around the house. Like the laundry, and the dishes, and waxing my mustache, and pooping. If the box says ages 4+, my four-year-old better be able to do it without my help. Because if I have to do every F'ing little thing with her, the box needs to say ages 40+.

6. Barbie dolls. I know I'm supposed to be against them because they give my daughter a false sense of a woman's body shape, but that's not what I'm worried about. My kid has no sense of negative self-image yet. If she did, she wouldn't be doing naked downward dog every night while I'm trying to get

her into a pull-up. Nope, I'll tell you who doesn't need to see hourglass Barbie bitches everywhere. Me. If I want to feel like shit about my body I just look in my full-length mirror. I don't need a nine-inch plastic doll to make me feel like a ~~hippotomus~~ ~~hippapotamus~~ (how the F do you spell this word?!) hippo.

7.   This toy:

Don't you dare buy this. I know it looks original and all, but I'll bet this is the kind of shit Jeffrey Dahmer got when he was a kid. I can already picture it. First my kid will be playing with this, and before you know it she'll be playing with the neighbor's cat carcass, and then one day the police will show up to take what

I thought was leftover meatballs out of my garage freezer but really it's our babysitter's head.

8.   And speaking of carcasses, stuffed animals. To say we don't need anymore is the understatement of the year. You know that game where there are a million stuffed animals in a big glass box and you have to steer the claw to try to pluck one out? Sometimes I feel like I live in that. One day I fully expect the claw to drop down through our skylight.

9.   Talking dolls. For one, they creep me the shit out. The way they talk without their lips moving like ventriloquists. Freeeaky. And here's another reason I can't stand them. Do you know what talking dolls say? Shit like, "Mommy, feed me," and "I wet myself, Mommy. Time for a diaper change!" This is the kind of crap I already hear like 40 times an hour from my own kids, so why in God's name would I want to hear more of that?

10. Horns, drums, cymbals, pianos, microphones, guitars, maracas, tambourines, bells, whistles, mp3 players, karaoke machines, sirens, rattles, buzzers, alarms, toys that beep, buzz, or have one of those annoying ladies who sings like she's all serious and shit like my middle school guitar-wielding music teacher.

That's it. Good luck out there! You're gonna F'ing need it.

Love and kisses,
Because I'm The Mom

The Truth, The Whole Truth, and None of The Bullshit You See on Pinterest

You know that moment when you're holding onto the parachute and walking around in a circle and all the kiddos in the middle are smiling (except for that one kid who always cries) and you're singing Pop Goes the Weasel and you can't help but think, WTF has my life come to?

HOW TO HOLD A MOMLYMPICS

So last year I'm sitting in front of my TV set watching the Olympics when Usain Bolt comes on and runs his little race and my hubby is all like, "Holy crap did you see that?! He is so amazing!" And I'm like, "Yeah, he is," but I'm totally bullshitting him because really I'm like, "Whatevs, that's nothing. Have you seen some of the shit moms do on a daily basis?" I mean I'd like to see Usain Bolt push a baseball through his penis (the best male equivalent to giving birth I could think of).

Anyways, it made me think. Who the hell cares if Michael Phelps can swim across a pool at like warp speed? Or that some sixteen-year-old waif can spell the entire Chinese alphabet with a stupid ribbon on a stick above her head? You know who's holding this world together and leaping buildings in a single bound every day? Moms, that's who. So this year when the weather's nice, I'm gonna hold a little event in my backyard. Dah Dah Dah Dahhhhhh! Ladies and gentlemen, Moms and Dads, Rug Rats of all ages, welcome to, drumroll please, the Molympics!!!

Just to give you a feel for what the Momlympics are all about, here are a few of the events:

Event 1: Hair-doing

MOM: Stay still so I can do your hair!

DAUGHTER: F.U. Mom, I just chugged a Red Bull!

In this event each mom will be challenged to put her daughter's hair into a ponytail while her daughter is jumping on a pogo stick after chugging a Red Bull. Up and down and up and down and falling off, all while Mom attempts to put her hair up. First one to get all of the hair into a reasonable ponytail wins this event.

Event 2: Food-cutting

CHILD: Wahhhhhhhhhhhhhhhhhhhhhhhhhhhhhhhhhhhhhh!

What's that the sound of? That's your little poop machine crying his head off because you can't prepare his food fast enough. In this event you will be given a bagful of grapes and a dull plastic knife. First mom to quarter every grape wins! And while you do it, you will be subjected to the grating sounds of a crying baby, either from an iPod or a real crying baby. TBD.

Event 3: Cheerio explosion

Moms, take your marks. Get set. Go! There are thousands of Cheerios spread throughout the yard. The moms will have thirty seconds to gather as many Cheerios as possible using nothing but her hands to collect them. There are no rules. Kicking, wrestling, tackling, grabbing, pulling, whatever you need to do to come out with more Cheerios than any other mom and prove your momlihood. You thought mud-wrestling was bad? You ain't seen nothin'.

Event 4: Blowout Bonanza

For the love of God, stop wriggling!!! It's just one of many things you'll hear screamed during this event where each mom is given a greased pig covered in poop. She must clean the pig with only three baby wipes and then outfit the squirming pig in a fresh diaper. The winner will receive a lifetime supply of Purell. All of which she will use that day.

Event 5: Poop poop pee doop

She who poops the fastest wins. I shit you not. Moms will each go into a restroom and a timer will start the second the door closes. Don't come out 'til you're done. And to make it realistic, someone will be banging on the door and yelling, "Mommmm!" the entire time. Contestants must have a smart phone with a camera to provide proof so as not to subject the referee (me) to any unnecessary odors.

Event 6: Beginners breastfeeding

Last one to take the battery charger clamps off her nipples wins!

So brush up on your skills and practice practice practice because one of you will soon win the Momlympics and be anointed *Mom of the Year!* Yeah, I'll bet you thought Gwenyth Paltrow or Oprah or someone like that handed this shit out. Well, you're wrong. I do.

(Before kids)

(After kids)

WHY I'M A WORSE MOM THAN YOU

Fifteen things I do as a Mom that will make you feel better about yourself:

1. If the kids spill a little milk and I'm too lazy to get a paper towel, I wipe it up with my sleeve. Or my foot if I'm wearing a sock.

2. Sometimes when I don't know where a toy goes, I just throw it away. Especially doll clothes. We have a lot of naked dolls in our house.

3. Speaking of naked, sometimes I take pictures of my kids' tiny tushies because I know I'm going to miss them one day. If someone were to open up iPhoto on my computer, I'd be arrested for pedophilia.

4. Last week I accidentally left the baby gate open and found my thirteen-month-old standing at the top of the stairs just staring down them. I think he was there for about 40 seconds before I showed up.

5. If the kids are crying too much at night sometimes I just give them Tylenol with blind hope that it fixes whatever is wrong.

6. When I want a bite of my daughter's food, I lie and tell her I have to check and make sure it's not poisonous.

7. Speaking of lies, sometimes I lie and say I have stomach upset just to get a few minutes to myself. Especially when I get a new People magazine. I call it FIBS (Fake Irritable Bowel Syndrome).

8. I've practically given up on finding the kids' nails when I cut them. I do a half-assed search and hope the vacuum cleaner gets the rest, even if I'm not vacuuming for two weeks. Or more.

9. Sometimes I realize I've been looking at my cell phone for the past ten minutes and haven't once looked up at my kids.

10. I'm so bad at geography I'm already worried about when my kids take it in school and they discover that I don't know where all the states are in the United States.

11. Back when I nursed, there were times I'd drink a glass or two of wine in hopes that it would help my son sleep better.

12. In the supermarket I hand my kids random items to occupy them (i.e. a package of straws or a jar of sprinkles) and then I leave those items all over the store when they get bored and I have to give them something new.

13. When I find a Cheerio on the ground at home if I don't have pockets or a trashcan, I just eat it. Provided it's not mushy or covered in fuzz. Or one of those small, hard ones that was once in someone's mouth.

14. Once there was a time I forgot to seatbelt my baby daughter into her infant car seat and we drove five blocks before I realized it.

15. I'm thankful for a lot of things, but mostly the speckled countertops in our kitchen so I can't tell how dirty they really are.

I don't know what they're serving for snack at school today, sweetie. At home I'm serving mimosas.

A LETTER TO MY DAUGHTER IN THE FUTURE, BUT NONE OF THAT SAPPY CRAP YOU SEE ON HUFF POST

To my daughter when she turns 18 (many many years from now),

Well, hey there kiddo. Remember me, the mom you used to love but now probably hate with every bone in your teenage body. If you're anything like the little shit I was at that age, you're barely speaking to me right now, much less listening to my brilliant words of wisdom.

The way I see it I'll be hitting menopause at about the same time you're in the thick of puberty so basically we're F'ed, so I figured I better write you this letter now before we're not speaking to each other. Then again if I'm wrong and we're like totally besties, I'll just tell you this shit over a pint of Ben and Jerry's and give you this letter so you'll have it in writing too.

Before you move away from home (at which point I'll be locked up in the bathroom drowning my tears in a bottle of vodka) I wanted to make sure to pass along some words of advice to you. Here are a few things to do in your early adulthood before life sucks the life out of you:

Get shitfaced once in a while. Some of my best bonding moments were when I had one (translation: four) too many cocktails with my girl friends. Just don't do any of the following while you're shitfaced: walk home alone, drive drunk or sleep with a guy. Even if he's like ridiculously hot. No, not because he might turn out to be fugly when you're sober. Consider this shit, if he's *that* attractive, guess what else might be attracted to him. Herpes, genital warts and crabs. Going home with a hangover the next morning is doable. Going home with the Red Lobster menu crawling all over your hoo-ha not so much.

And while we're on the subject of bonding, try to make a lot of great friends in your twenties. Here are a few things that happen when you're a young adult: you go out a lot, you drink, and you hang out on people's couches. As you get older these things happen less and less. Not that you can't bond with a friend over a stinky diaper change. It just doesn't quite bring you together the same way dropping your pants to pee in an alley does. Not that I've done that.

And speaking of dropping your pants, let's talk about your career choice. Yeah, picking something you love is important, but here's some shit the career counselors won't tell you. You know how you say one day you want to get married and have babies and all that junk and give me little grandbabies I can cuddle and love and hand back to you when they take a shit? If you can, pick a job that's going to be flexible with hours one day and let you work from home. There's no such thing as a part time investment banker. Or a part time cardiac surgeon. They're fabulous jobs and yeah, I'd be proud as hell to say my daughter is doing a heart transplant, but I'd also be watching your kiddo all day, and I'm not sure how cool it would be for me to walk into your OR and say, "Here, take your rug rat. He just made a doodie and I ain't changing it."

Notice how in that last paragraph I said *you want to get married one day*. I didn't say you want to find a husband. Yeah, if you're a lesbian, just tell us. Don't beat around the bush. Wait, yes, beat around the bush but tell us you're beating around the bush. It'll actually make us feel better, especially your dad who has a gun ready for the first guy who asks for your hand in marriage.

Which is a great segue to dating. Whether you're into men or women, you're going to date a bunch of assholes along the way. They might break up with you in a text message or cheat on you with their ex who they broke up with in a text message. And they'll probably make you cry and feel like crapola. Just know that they are not a waste of time. They are all there to teach you what you DON'T want in a partner.

Because one day your boobs will droop so low they touch your ankles, and your elbows will make you wonder whether you're ¼ elephant, and your eyesight will be so bad you'll fail to notice your one-haired goatee until it gets tangled in your necklace, and that's when you'll want a partner who's not going to throw up in their mouth a little when they see you naked. You want to end up with someone who thinks you're more gorgeous than the day you first met.

And one last thing. Even if you're not talking to me right now, know that you can always tell me anything. ANYTHING. I've probably been there myself, even if I never told you about it. I might want to kick the shit out of you and lock you in a room forever, but I won't actually do it. I will always be there for you (with a bottle of something hard if you're 21 or a pint of something chocolatey if you're not).

I love you.
XOXOXOXOXOXOXO
Love,
Mommy (Of course I realize by now you're probably calling me Mom. Or shithead.)

I love when I blow my nose while I'm peeing. Not only am I multitasking, but the pee comes out faster so I'm saving time. Awesome.

A LETTER TO MY SON IN THE FUTURE, YOU KNOW, IF HE HASN'T DISOWNED ME FOR THIS BOOK

To my son when he turns eighteen (a lonnnnnng time from now),

Hey, little buddy. Can I still call you that even though you tower over me now? BTW, I appreciate you not saying anything about my gray roots, that is if you're saying anything at all to me these days. The truth is I don't know jack shit about boys since I came from a houseful of mostly vajayjays, so who the F knows whether they talk to their moms or not when they're teenagers.

So as you pack your bags (or more likely as I pack your bags) to head off to college (dear God pleeeeease let it be a local one or you might find me curled up in one of your boxes), I hope you don't mind but I've pulled together a list of shit you SHOULDN'T do while you're there. Sure, I should totally take you fishing or some crap like that and tell you this to your face, but screw that. I'd be embarrassed, you'd be embarrassed, and this way you can pin this letter above your extra long twin-sized bed so you'll never forget. Okay, I'm just gonna dive right in here.

Don't ever sleep with a girl without a condom on. Not just protection. A CONDOM!!! I don't give a rat's ass if she says she's on the pill or wearing a diaphragm (and if she says she's wearing a sponge, run like the wind 'cause that girl's not a girl, she's a dinosaur). Because here's what can happen when you don't wear a condom. You can get all kinds of shit. Like AIDS or herpes or chlamidia. I have no F'ing idea how to spell that word and I'm okay with that because anyone who knows how to spell chlamidia has probably had it. In fact, I will quiz you every time I see you to make sure you can't spell it.

Oh, and here's another thing you can get if you don't use a condom. A baby. That's right, a pooping, shitting, crying, peeing, never-sleeping, attached-to-its-ho-bag-mother baby. And believe me, you don't want one of those. I can't tell you how annoying babies are. Uhhh, except for you of course. Nahhh, even you were a pain in the ass.

Plus, if you get a girl preggers, you're going to be her daddy-slave FOREVAHHH. And I know some hot little chica might look awesome now in her Vic's Secret panties that say "call me" on the crotch, but really that's just a sneak peek into the irritating nag she's going to be if you get her preggers. "*Call me* when you're leaving the office. *Call me* in case I need you to pick up milk. *Call me* and tell me you love me. *Call me* when you're out with the guys. *Call me* just because I want your ass to be at my beckon call."

So I cannot say this enough. Do not get a girl preggers. Do not get a girl preggers. Do not get a girl preggers. Do not get a girl preggers. Do not get a girl preggers. Do not get a girl preggers. Do not get a girl preggers. Do not get a girl preggers. Do not get a girl preggers. Do not get a girl preggers.

And while we're on the subject of getting laid (gasp! yes, your mama just said getting laid), if you don't really like a girl, like really really like her, don't spoon her. I know it seems like a stupid little thing, but there's like some weird switch in women and as soon as you spoon them, they start to picture things like the L word and marriage and shit like that. I know, it's weird. But women are weird. Duh, look at me.

Okay, so let's move on to a different subject. While you're in college, I probably don't have to tell you this, but it's okay to drink your face off once in a while. And there are lots of fun, harmless things to do while you're shitfaced. Like swallow a goldfish (I know all the PETA people reading this are like WTF, but seriously people, it's a goldfish). Or come up with some annoying accent with your friends and annoy the shit out of everyone around you all night while you talk like that. Or pass out and have your friends draw with Sharpies all over you. Does it suck waking up with a Hitler mustache? Sure. But it's important to laugh at yourself once in a while.

But here's the real reason I'm talking to you about getting shitfaced. Here are some things NOT to do while you're tanked. Get in the car and drive somewhere. If you are drunk and need to get from point A to point B, call me. Go ahead and say you're at your drug dealer's and you're going to a whorehouse. I don't give a shit, just call me. I will come drive you there because I would rather do that than let you drive drunk.

And here's another thing NOT to do while you're drunk. Get into a fistfight at a bar. Because here's what happens to a-holes who fight in bars. They die. Or they get thrown in jail and they have to call their parents to bail them out and their parents kill them and guess what. They die.

And last but not least, one last thing not to do when you get shitfaced (Side note, I LOVE that spell check totally recognizes the word shitfaced. It doesn't recognize dreidel but it does recognize shitfaced.

WTF?). Anyways, last but not least, when you're shitfaced do not get a girl preggers!!!

Aww shit, this letter is like a novel already so let me just rattle off a few more. Don't forget to wash your sheets sometimes, at least once a semester, especially if you're busy NOT getting girls pregnant in them. Don't pick a girl for her boobs because one day they will be around her ankles. And don't forget to hug me when you come home to visit. Every single weekend.

I love you and will be drowning my sorrows in red wine until I see you again on Friday when you come home to hug me.

Love,
Yo mama

P.S. Just in case you skimmed this letter because it's too long and just read the last line, do not get a girl preggers.

Okay, I know a bunch of those perfect moms say that love is cooking a three-course meal for your family and shit like that, but I'll tell you what love is. Love is when you call the pediatrician's office to ask about the symptoms of a UTI and the nurse tells you to check your daughter's pee to see if it smells foul, and then you practically bury your nose in her pull-up or in the still steaming toilet water and take a deep whiff. That, my friends, is love.

I DON'T READ NO STINKIN' PARENTING MAGAZINES

So the other day I was reading some sappy crap on Huff Post when they started talking about helicopter parenting and I was like WTF is that so I decided to look it up. Holy shit, there's like a name for every kind of parent out there. Who the hell knew?! Well, probably half of you because you read parenting books and shit, but all I ever read is People magazine so I had no idea.

Anyways, it's kind of like how ten years ago everyone was trying to figure out which Sex and the City character they were. I was like Carrie but fatter and with a little Miranda and Samantha mixed in but ZERO Charlotte. But I digress. So as soon as I see this parenting styles list, I scan it to see which of these styles I am.

Not me. Not me. Not me. Not me. Not me.

Awesome, so basically I don't fit in anywhere and I belong on the island of misfits. What else is new? So here goes. My very scientific analysis of the five different parenting styles and why I'm not any of them.

Instinctive Parenting

Definition: This is when parents pretty much just go with their gut and listen to their instincts as they raise their kids.

Uhhhh, yeah, this one is not me. Like right now as I type this, my four-year-old is purposely running as loudly as possible down the hallway either trying to imitate a herd of elephants or attempting to wake her napping brother, and you know what my gut is telling me? Go the F out there and kill her.

If parents like me went with our instincts, we would all murder our kids sometime between the ages of 2 and 4 and the human race would eventually die out. What killed the dinosaurs? An asteroid. What killed the humans? Instinctive parenting.

That's why they literally teach you at the hospital before you leave to never shake a baby. Because at some point when your poop machine is screaming at the top of her lungs no matter how much you swaddle her, sing to her or bounce her on an exercise ball, instinct tells you to shake the F'ing baby.

Attachment parenting

Definition: These parents are all about answering to their children's every need like ASAP. And they're into shit like the family bed, homeschooling and that regurgitation crap Alicia Silverstone did with her kid (Remember when she fed him chewed up kale like a bird right out of her mouth? Blagggh, I won't even eat kale *before* it's chewed up by someone else).

So here's what I think of this one. Unless you just randomly opened this book right now to this page to see if you want to buy it (you do) you probably know that I'm like the complete opposite of attachment parenting. I mean this is what I said when we moved to our neighborhood. "WTF do you mean it's only half-day kindergarten?!"

And these attachment parenters choose to have their kids home ALLLLLLLL day. And not just plopped down in front of the TV. I mean just the thought of having my kids at home all day every day for the next 16 years makes me want to stab my brain with two screwdrivers, one through each ear.

After having them at home all day teaching them shit like Algebra that you can't remember how to do so you have to relearn it, you have to let them curl up with you in your bed at night too? No thank you. I mean my husband and I have a king-sized bed so that we don't have to touch someone else's skin while we sleep, so the thought of being jabbed by some little rug rat's elbow in the eyeball in the middle of the night is just not cool.

And what about sex? Can you imagine? We're doing it in the laundry room or the basement at 3 AM because all the kids are in our bed, and one of them starts calling, "MOMMMMMYY, I want some cheese!!!!" And I have to be like, "Hold that orgasm, honey, I've gotta go unwrap some Velveeta for poop machine #2 right this very second because I'm an attachment parenter. I'll be right back."

Helicopter Parenting

Definition: Helicopter parents hover over their kids like a helicopter (duh) basically doing everything for them and constantly making sure they don't get hurt.

Hmmm, yeahh, as if I don't have enough shit of my own to do, I'm going to go ahead and do everything my kid is supposed to do too. WTF? You know what happens to these kids? They're in college and Mommy's still doing everything for them.

ME: Awwww, darn it guys, I can't go to pilates today. Holden just texted me and I have to run by the dorm to wipe his ass. He just made poopies.

Authoritative Parenting

Definition: These are parents who expect their kids to follow the rules they make, but when the kids stray, the parents tend to be more supportive than punishing.

Bwahahahaha! Okay, I have two things to say about this. First of all, I'm not stupid enough to think my kids are going to follow my rules. I mean, my kid's the one who outlined every corner in our house with a purple crayon. And the kid who wiped poop on her nightstand last week. And the kid who purposely spilled her yogurt down the heating vent.

And second of all, you want me to do WHAT? Be supportive and NOT punish her ass for this stuff? I'm like sit the F down in that corner young lady, and you can get up when the timer goes off, and then I go set the timer for two years. But apparently I'm supposed to speak sternly to her and then go enroll her in art class or something. I have three words to say about this. F that shit.

Permissive Parenting

Definition: These are the totally badass awesome parents who bought us kegs and shit in high school and taught us how to make Jello so we could make Jello shots. They act more like friends and less like parents and don't really discipline their kids.

Okay, so I already have enough friends and even if I were looking for more, I'm not sure I would pick my kids. I mean my kids can be total a-holes (duh, check out the title of the book), and would you be friends with someone who pees on you in the shower and throws the perfectly good dinner you cooked across the room?

ME: Wow, Jen, your potato salad sucks balls. But it makes an awesome Frisbee.

And here's another thing, hell if I'm going to give away my alcohol. I mean, yes, sometimes I bring my friends bottles of wine and shit like that, but they return the favor. But where the hell is my sixteen-year-old going to buy *me* a six-pack? 'Cause Tarjay cards like anyone under the age of 97. I know because I was all psyched when my best bud Arnie carded me last week there and I was all excited that he thought I looked under 21 until he explained to me that they pretty much have to card anyone who breathes. Dude, Arnie, we're supposed to be friends. Just act like you think I look 20, capiche?

So there you go. All five parenting styles. So which one are you? One of the Baby-shakers, Codependent granolaheads, Nervous nellies, Dicktators, or Enabling A-Holes? I mean, not that there's anything wrong with any of them. Basically the way I see it, we're all just doing whatever it F'ing takes to survive and not go to prison for killing a child and not raise someone who will go to prison for killing a child. Right?

I love when those annoyingly perfect moms brag that they ONLY give their kids all-natural shit. You know what's all-natural? Poisonous berries and 'shrooms.

MOM'S SERENITY PRAYER

God, grant me the Serenity to accept the things I cannot change (that 4-year-olds are a-holes);

Courage to change the things I can (the clock so I can put her to bed earlier);

And Wisdom to know the difference (between scolding and unleashing every curse word I know on her).

Living one day at a time (until my husband comes home so I can dump her ass on him);

Enjoying one moment at a time (that precious few seconds when she has her brother in a headlock and it's totally quiet);

Accepting hardship as the pathway to peace (at 8 pm when I can finally shut the bathroom door and poop and read People magazine all by myself);

Taking, as He did, this sinful world as it is (children born with vocal cords),

Not as I would have it (children's vocal cords surgically removed);

Trusting that He will make all things right (that one day she will have her own daughter—karma!),

If I surrender to His Will (waving the white flag from the three-week-old fort I'm not allowed to take down in the living room);

That I may be reasonably happy in this life (define reasonably),

And supremely happy with Him (as long a there are cheeseburgers and foot massages and no 4-year-olds, I'm happy to sport a perma-grin),

Forever in the next (whoa whoa whoa, forever is like some serious commitment, but WTH).

Amen.

There's no place like home. Unless you have kids, in which case there's no place like a bar.

This Is A Really Short Chapter About Girl Scout Cookies Because Girl Scout Cookies Are So F'ing Awesome They Deserve Their Own Chapter

Yayyy, our Girl Scout cookies arrived! Boooo, our Girl Scout cookies arrived. See, not only do they make me gain weight, but they make me think like a schizophrenic.

I think it's F'ing hysterical that they call them THIN Mints. A more appropriate name might be Lard-Ass Mints. Fine, I guess the cookie itself is thin. Maybe that's why I can eat like nine of them in one bite.

This is the conversation I just had with myself.

ME: Ohhhh, I really want a Girl Scout cookie.

ME: Don't do it. You want to be skinny, don't you?

ME: Yeah, but I really really want it.

ME: Which lasts longer? One cookie, or being skinny?

ME: Yeah, you're right.

(ten seconds later)

ME: I still want it. I'm having it. One cookie can't hurt.

ME: That'd be true if you could have just one.

ME: (mouth full) Fuck you.

Have you ever noticed that thin mints don't taste as good as they used to? Like 27 cookies ago they were absolutely delicious.

Awww shit, I just HAD to grab a thin mint before getting ready for bed. Now I either have to wait a long time to brush my teeth or my spit's gonna be all brown.

When a sweet little innocent Girl Scout comes to my door and says, "They're only $4," do you know what I say? "Bullshit." Because I'm going to eat that whole F'ing box and then I'm going to have to go buy more transition jeans at Tarjay, and we all know that when you go to Tarjay it is physically impossible to spend less than $100, so really one box of Girl Scout cookies costs me $104.

DISNEY AND CAILLOU AND OTHER ANNOYING CRAP I WANT TO CRAP ON

IF CAILLOU WERE A REAL PERSON I'D GLADLY GO TO JAIL FOR KILLING HIM

I love how the experts tell us if we're gonna let our kids watch TV we should watch it with them. WHAT?!!! Why on earth do you think I'm putting her in front of the TV in the first place, Mr. So-called Expert? To get some shit done. So yes, sometimes some inappropriate shows slip between the cracks when I'm not looking. No, not shows like Free My Willy and Batman in Robin. Shows like Caillou. Not Blow me Caillou or Caillou goes to the local Whorehouse. Just Caillou. Because Caillou sucks and can eat my shorts and I hate his F'ing guts.

Now if you've never seen Caillou, you might be inclined to watch it to see WTF I'm talking about. Well don't. This is not like one of those times when I tell you NOT to do a Google image search of placenta artwork but I know you're going to just because I said don't. I am 200% dead serious when I say, DON'T WATCH CAILLOU. You will hate it, you will hate me, and most of all you will hate him. Wanna know why? Here are ten GIANT reasons I hate Mother-F'ing Caillou:

1. What the hell kind of name is Caillou? The only people who can pull off names that weird are really good-looking people. People like Hermione. But two-dimensional, round-headed bald kids? Not so much. Ordinarily I'm crazy lazy (Uggh, I hate

when I inadvertently rhyme) but since I'm writing about him I decided to look up his name. Apparently Caillou is French for pebble. Well, there you go. He is about as lame as a rock.

2. Why is he bald? I've heard a lot of people joke that he has cancer. Because you know, leukemia is so funny. But seriously, someone once told me that by not giving him a hair color, all kids could relate to him' blondes, brunettes, redheads. What?! That makes about no sense at all. Then why not give him hair in ALL different colors? Or clear hair? How many four-year-olds have *no* hair? None. Well, maybe kids with alopecia, but if that's what they're going for then have an episode about it or something.

3. Caillou has the most annoying theme song in the history of television. As if we haven't heard him say "I'm Caillou" enough times throughout the song, he says it like 9 times at the end of it. "I'm Caillou, Caillou, Caillou, Caillou, Caillou, Caillou, Caillou." For the love of God, stop singing! We know who the F you are already. The show is named after you for Pete's sake.

4. I'm inventing a new drinking game. Whenever Caillou whines you take a drink. The last person to get their stomach pumped wins. And once your kid watches Caillou, it's not just Caillou's whiny-ass voice you have to listen to. Your kid starts to sound like that too. Remember the scene in Reservoir Dogs when the guy gets his ear cut off? Sometimes I wish that were me.

5. I'll tell you what really irks me. The way the narrator calls Caillou's mom "Mommy," like it's actually her name. The narrator says crap like, "Mommy is very good at making

Caillou feel better." The only person who should call someone Mommy is the kid who came out of her vajayjay. Period. I know some husbands do it too, but they shouldn't. It's wrong for so many reasons.

6.   The narrator is so F'ing annoying she gets #6 too. Have you ever noticed how she's constantly cutting in to say things like, "Caillou felt sad." No shit Sherlock, he's crying.

7.   What is up with all the dowdy moms on this show? Like Caillou's mom (see how that works, narrator?). Not only does she dress like she's 9,000 years old, she constantly looks like she's free-balling. Did the illustrator forget to draw a bra on her? And if this show is all about characters we can relate to, is she supposed to look like me? Talk about insulting. Do I walk around with my muffin top protruding beneath my shirt? No. I do what all the mothers do. I squish it into my jeans where no one can see it.

8.   Musical interludes. 'Nuff said.

9.   Why is he bald? Yes, I know I already did this one, but it's so annoying I think it merits being mentioned again.

10.   I'm trying to think of one more thing to make this list an even ten, but I'm totally distracted. All I can think about is getting a snack right now. It's 4:43 so I can't put dinner on the table for 17 more minutes. The 17 longest minutes of my life. Besides when I'm watching Caillou.

Half the characters on Mickey Mouse aren't wearing pants, and yet the way we can tell if they're guys or girls is whether they have eyelashes and bows. WTF?

Oh hello anatomically correct doll that should never have been created. Here are a few things I think about you:

1. There's one thing and one thing only that plastic penises should be made for. And a baby doll ain't it.

2. Can't you totally hear the conversation when they were designing this doll?

    DESIGNER 1: Whatta you think? Circumcised?

DESIGNER 2: Nahhh, I was thinking he should have that straight-out-of-the-womb look.

DESIGNER 1: Bloody and covered in a cheese-like substance?

DESIGNER 2: Gross, no. I just meant uncircumcised.

DESIGNER 1: But isn't it healthier if it's snipped?

DESIGNER 2: Dude, it's a plastic doll.

DESIGNER 1: Good point. Uncircumcised it is.

3. Look at that itty bitty ballsack (ball sac??? ball sack??? The Internet spells it like 9 different ways). I can't help but be a little jealous of this baby's mom who doesn't have to hire a crane operator to lift his scrotum (insert heebie jeebies emoticon here) out of the way when she changes a nasty poopie diaper.

4. If they were going for realistic, shouldn't it be erect the way they are like 90% of the time when you're changing them?

5. So most dolls just have a weird smooth, hill-like area where the genitalia should be, kind of like a faceless mannequin. Totally weird, but for some reason this attempt to make a plastic baby penis is even more disturbing. I know the Supreme Court is busy, but can't they just take like five minutes and write a law that says all plastic dolls must be wearing painted on underwear?

6. I'll bet a plastic penis is so much easier to clean than a skin one. And that it doesn't get those gross hairs wrapped around

it sometimes that make you feel like a pedophile while you're picking them off.

7.   If I wanted a plastic penis, I'd go to Times Square, not my kid's toy box.

Guess I should have given hubby a BJ after all. Look who I found in our bed this morning. And she soooo has sex hair.

CALLING DR. SNOW WHITE, DDS

So a couple of months ago I decided it was probably time for Zoey to have her first dentist appointment. I know she was supposed to start at age three, but A. I've been busy, and B. she's going to lose those stupid teeth one day anyway so why waste a lot of time on them when she pretty much gets a do-over at age six, and C. WTF is a dentist going to do for a three-year-old besides charge us a boatload of money?

I know every dentist and hygienist (damn, that's a hard word to spell) reading this wants to jump through the F'ing page and beat the crap out of me for saying that, so I'm sorry. I promise that if I win the lottery or find an oil well in our backyard, I will take Holden to the dentist when he's three.

Anyways, I'm looking at dentists online and their pictures are popping up when Zoey walks in.

ZOEY: Who's that?

ME: I'm looking for a dentist for you.

ZOEY: I want one that looks like a princess.

Ummm, yeah, that is exactly what you should look for in a dentist, kiddo. Good looks. Not where they went to school or how close is their office or whether they're open on weekends. Nope, looks are definitely first priority. Although truth be told, I was intentionally looking at the pictures because I wanted to find someone who's not a dinosaur and going to retire in like three years. But okay, I'll start looking for one that looks more like Rapunzel or Ariel.

Do you know where she gets this shit? Yeah, you know. Dis to the Mother-F'ing Ney. Uhhh, sorry, that's like my lame attempt at being cool and totally doesn't make sense. Yeah, Disney has single-handedly taught my kiddo that being good-looking is like the be-all end-all.

Like the other day I was reading one of those Little Golden books to Zoey about Beauty and the Beast. Ahhh, it actually is such a beautiful story. This totally hot-to-trot, book-loving bittie falls in love with this guy who looks like he needs a nose job, a wax job and a visit to the chiropractor. She falls in love with him for everything he is on the inside. And then when he's dying, she kisses him and says I love you and she saves his life with her undying love. Awesome. Amazing. Shedding a tear. End of story. Ennhhh, wrong.

Nooo, Disney can't leave it there. God forbid someone isn't good-looking in one of their stories. So at the end of the book Mr. Beast suddenly transforms into a runway model (although not half as good-looking as Flynn Rider if you ask me). I actually thought about ripping this last page out of the book, but then the page before it would be gone too and the story would end with Gaston plunging a knife into the Beast's back. And Gaston's an F'ing asshole so I'm not giving him the pleasure.

And this Disney crap doesn't stop with Beauty and the Beast. The other day I was reading about Merida, you know the princess from Brave who's like the only normal princess. I mean that's the kind of girl I'd like to shoot the shit with over a margarita. The kind of girl who's not perfect and takes like 9,000 hours to straighten her hair sometimes. I'd be like, "Heyyy, did you straighten your hair? It looks good," and she'd be like, "Yeah, I got it blown out the other day at my haircut so I haven't showered in like 6 days or else it'll get all frizzy again."

Anyways, I was reading the other day that Disney is changing her to look more like a sexpot. Her shirt is cut lower, her hair is lustrous curls instead of a frizzy mess, and either she's wearing a corset or she went on the Atkins diet because just a couple of weeks ago her waist was like two inches bigger. You know what I would like to see just once? A Disney princess whose weight yo-yos like a normal person.

ARIEL: What up Cinderella, have you been working out?

CINDERELLA: Uh-huh, I'm doing that PX-90 workout. It's awesome, but I have to stop since I pulled my hammy yesterday and now I'm totally gonna gain it all back.

So yeah, apparently Merida wasn't sexpotty enough (hmmm, sexpotty. I wonder if Kohler makes one of those), so they've brought her from like a four up to like an eight. Let's face it, Merida, you'll never be a Jasmine.

But it's shit like this that's making my daughter want the dentist she sees for ten minutes a year to look like a princess.

So you're probably wondering what I did. Well, first I explained to her that it doesn't matter what your dentist looks like, or anyone for that matter, while she looked at me like I was INSANE IN THE BRAIN. So you know what I did? I called the ugliest dentist I could find. Not. Sadly I pictured her going to the dentist for the first time and FREAKING THE

SHIT OUT and digging her claws into me as I pinned her down to the chair as the homely dentist held her mouth open with a vice grip or some shit like that. Fine, whatever, let's make this trip as easy as possible. So I called the only pretty female dentist I could find in the area. Guess who's going on maternity leave and not coming back.

So I did what any sane mother would do. I found the one who looked most like a prince. Why hello, Dr. Hotty Hot Pants. Holy crap, talk about irony—her dentist is total eye candy. So as he examined Zoey, I examined his face, and his ass, and his biceps. And I prayed he'd come over after and examine my mouth. With his tongue. You know, because looks don't matter.

Disney movies are all about our kids' fantasies coming true, right? Toys coming to life, girls becoming princesses, animals talking, parents dying. WTF?

5 little monkeys jumping on the bed
One fell off and bumped his head
Mama called the doctor and the doctor said
No more monkeys jumping on the bed.

4 little monkeys jumping on the bed
One fell off and bumped his head
Mama gave him an eye-roll and said, "See?"
No more monkeys jumping on the bed.

3 little monkeys jumping on the bed
One fell off and bumped his head
Mama used restraint and spoke through gritted teeth, "Do it again and I'm taking away all of your bananas and you're getting a time out."
No more monkeys jumping on the bed.

2 little monkeys jumping on the bed
One fell off and bumped his head
Mama finally lost it and went ballistic on his ass. "WTF are you doing? Do you not F'ing listen to any of the shit I say? What part of do not jump on the bed do you not F'ing understand?!
No more goddamn monkeys jumping on the bed!!!!"

1 little monkey jumping on the bed
He fell off and bumped his head
Mama took one look at him and said, "Serves you right, kiss your own F'ing boo-boo. Mama needs some wine. Is it four o'clock yet? WTH, it is somewhere."

ME: *If you see a gun, you get away and go find a grownup.*
ZOEY: *Or a knight.*
ME: *Yes, by all means. If you are in the 1600s, go find a knight.*

SOMEDAY MY GAY
PRINCE WILL COME

Holy crap, have you ever been to a Disney on Ice show? Me neither. Wait, no, that's a total lie. I was just too embarrassed to admit it. It's basically hell on earth only it's really cold.

DUMBASS ME: Heyyyy, I'll bet Zoey would LOVE Disney on Ice. I'm going to spend 9 million dollars and buy some tickets.

SHIT FOR BRAINS HUBBY: Great idea, but aren't there any cheap seats?

DUMBASS ME: Those are the cheap seats.

So I bought the tickets and was so excited I told Zoey about it right away.

DUMBASS ME: Guess where we're going?!

ZOEY: Where?!

DUMBASS ME: Disney on Ice!

ZOEY: Yipppppeeeeee! I'm going to get my shoes on!

Whoopsies.

DUMBASS ME: Uhhh, it's not 'til Feburary.

Are we going today? Are we going today? Are we going today? Are we going today? Are we going today? Are we going today? Are we going today? Times 180 until 6 months later when it was finally time to go.

Oh my Zoey, you look absolutely amazingly adorable in your gorgeous dress-up gown THAT'S NOT EVEN ONE OF THE F'ING DISNEY PRINCESSES!!! Are you shitting me? I told her she could wear a princess dress and this is the one she chose?! Here are the Disney dresses we own: Snow White, Rapunzel, Belle, Belle, Belle (that's not a typo, we actually own three Belle dresses), Minnie Mouse, Dorothy, Merida, and Ariel. But she chose to wear some giant ball gown someone sent us that's sure to take up two seats at the show. And there goes her chance of being picked out of the audience to stand on the stage with the princesses. Not that I really wanted that. But I kinda secretly did. And how the F am I supposed to clean that thing if she gets $12 snow cone on it? I shit you not, I paid $12 for ice.

So anyways, we're sitting there in the audience when the lights went down and the music started. Now I have a confession to make. A big one. Worse than admitting that I like the Bachelorpad. Worse than admitting that I have hair on my toes. Worse than admitting that sometimes I stand in front of the mirror topless and lift my arms to see what my boobs used to look like.

Okay, here goes. I cry at everything Disney. Yeah yeah yeah, I know that sometimes I paint myself as this heartless, cynical bitch, but really I am the person who tears up on *It's a Small World* at DisneyWorld. It's mortifying. I cry the moment I see Cinderella's castle. I cry the second I hear Aladdin's *A Whole New World*. Hell, I even cry when the pilot announces, "Welcome to Orlando." So I expected to be a bawling hot mess by the middle of Disney on Ice.

And then the show began. And here's what was going through my head. Don't cry, don't cry, don't cry, don't cry, wait I'm not gonna cry because this is stupid as shit. Umm, these skaters kind of suck ass. I mean I wasn't expecting Olympics level skating but maybe a little bit. And holy crap, Aladdin just dropped Jasmine on her face! Okay, I'm kind of crying in pain if that counts.

And just when I thought it couldn't get any worse, the grand finale happened. You know how at the end of a July 4th celebration there's an onslaught of fireworks? Disney on Ice was the same thing, only it was an explosion of princesses. I shit you not. It was like the curtain was projectile-vomiting every Disney princess you can imagine. Cinderella, Snow White, Tiana, Jasmine (with a bandage on her face), Ariel, Aurora, Etcetera (ahhh, wasn't Etcetera the most beautiful princess of all?).

They were all spinning around the ice with their princes to the song *Someday my Prince Will Come*, and while usually I would be tearing up right now and blowing my nose into an overused crusty snot rag, I started to have a totally different feeling— holy crap, this is bullshit. *Someday my prince will come?* Sitting there next to my daughter I wanted to stand up and scream, "Yo, Disney, are you F'ing kidding me?! This is the crap we want to teach our daughters?!!!"

It's not the fact that I don't want my daughter to be "rescued" by a man. It's the fact that she can be rescued or not rescued by whoever the F she chooses. So as I was watching alllllllllll of these princesses with their princes skating around the rink, I was like, "Seriously, Disney, you can't make one measly little couple gay? Really? You have like 2,000 couples, so would it be such a big deal to hook up two princesses?"

I mean just think of the financial potential some girl-on-girl action could bring. Fathers would rush their families to the theaters to see a little tongue between Jasmine and Belle. Or what about Mulan? A hot Asian lipstick lesbian? Jessica Rabbit would be left in the dust. And you know what would be awesome? I'd like to see Prince Charming sing *Someday my Prince Will Come.*

Someday my gay prince will come,
Away to the Northeast we'll run,
Where a power couple we'll be,
Then adoption will make us three.

Someday when Spring is here,
No one will care if we're straight or queer,
They'll all see that our love is so kind,
Whether we do it in the front or behind,
Someday when my dreams come true.

Now that would make me tear up. So you know what, until that shit happens, I ain't going back to Disney on Ice. Woo-hoo, that should buy me a few years.

Sometimes I let Caillou babysit my kids. How F'ed up is that?

Annnnnd This Is What My Life Has Turned Into. Awesome.

You know what sucks? The fact that sleeping in the "wet spot" isn't from "doing it" anymore. It's because someone's diaper leaked in our bed.

BABIES R'N'T US

Awwww shit, the six-week, post-baby checkup. You know what that means? I have to have sex again. Uhhhh, I mean I get to make magnificent love to my adoring husband. Not that I don't enjoy sex. It's just that right now I'm kind of exhausted, breastfeeding, hormonal, in pain down there, want to murder him because he doesn't have to breastfeed, and did I mention exhausted? I mean I could literally fall asleep crowd-surfing at a Metallica concert, but you want me to waste valuable horizontal sleep time having sex? Besides, do you know what can happen when you have sex? You can get preggers. Been there done that. So anyways, this is what my six-week checkup was like.

OB: So what are you using for birth control?

ME: Our baby.

OB: (blank stare)

ME: Seriously, he's like constantly laying between us and cockblocking my husband.

OB: What about when your baby's not there?

ME: (blank stare)

OB: Have you thought about what you might want to use when he *does* start sleeping in his own room?

ME: I don't know, isn't there like some magic pill that I can take that will make me temporarily infertile?

OB: Yes, it's called the pill.

ME: Nahhh, F that shit. I have to remember to take it like every single day. I'm talking about ONE pill I can take and it'll make my whole system go kaput for a while.

OB: Yes, it's called the Kaput pill.

ME: Really?

OB: No, not really. What about a vasectomy?

I'm pretty sure she's suggesting this because she thinks I shouldn't breed anymore.

ME: I don't know, that's just so final. I mean my husband's 100% done but I'm only like 98%, so we'll probably have another. And yes, I know I'm 40 (quit looking at me like that, biatch), but didn't you see that lady who just had a baby at 62? So I ain't closing that door yet.

Yada yada yada, we discuss some of my choices, and here's my take on why a cockblocking baby is a better birth control choice for me than any of the options on the market:

IUD

So all of the sudden I have all these Mommy friends who are using IUDs and at first I was like, "Hmmm, that could be kinda cool," until I heard them all bitching about the little strings. The WHAT?!!! The little strings. Yeah, apparently these little strings hang out of your cervix and you're supposed to reach in there and check once in a while to make sure they're still there. I'm picturing a permanent tampon string in there, only there are two so it's like you accidentally put a second tampon in because you forgot there was already one in there. Grrr, I hate when that happens. Or maybe they're more like threads like when the hem of your sleeve has a little thread dangling off it and you try to rip it off but every time you pull it it just gets longer and you finally have to bite that shit off. Only these threads are dangling from your cervix, and I'd constantly want to rip them off so thank God I'm not flexible enough to bend over and bite them off with my teeth. And this is why I can never have an IUD.

Condoms

First of all, condoms cost like $9,000. Not really, but they cost money and I remember when there were like buckets of free ones in college (unless you went to some religiousy college where the teenagers with raging hormones practice abstinence, bwahahahahaha!). But seriously, paying for a condom each time I have sex makes me feel like I'm paying for sex, which is hilarious because these days you pretty much have to pay *me* to have sex. Hmmm, wait, does that make me a prostitute?

Plus, can we discuss the physical condom itself? You pop it on the tip of his peeper and you're like why the F won't this thing unroll? Unroll damn it! Forty seconds later, you figure it out. Awww shit, that sucker is upside down. Well, if that's not a buzz kill, I don't know what is. And once he's "done" with the condom, it's basically like a water balloon full of spluge that he tosses in the trashcan so the whole trashcan smells like sex. Awesome. Not.

Female condom

Do you know anyone who's ever used this? Nahhh, me neither. So I looked it up and here are some of the advantages to using a female condom— it's 95% effective (which basically means if you have sex 20 times, you'll get preggers, at least according to my F'ed up math). It's safe for anal sex (if you can handle the idea of putting a ring up your tush hole. I don't know why that sounds worse than putting a penis in there, but it does). And the outer ring may possibly stimulate the clitoris while you're having sex (so let me get this straight? Not only am I the one dealing with birth control, but now he doesn't even have to work hard to get me off?). Okay, so those are the *advantages* to using this method of birth control.

The way I see it, here is the biggest disadvantage to using a female condom—you have to say you use a female condom. Blagggh. I guess you can say you use a Fem-Con and make it sound a little cooler like Comic-Con, but then people will just ask you what a Fem-Con is and you'll have to whisper, "It's a female condom," and they'll laugh and think you're kidding, but then when they realize you're not kidding they'll stop laughing and look at you weird and think you're gross. No way ho zay.

A Diaphragm

There are two reasons I am not wearing an F'ing diaphragm (shit, that's a hard word to spell). 1. Aren't diaphragms only for people who were born in the 1950's? And 2. All I can picture is carrying the case around in my purse and then one day it falls out in front of the cashier at Tarjay and she sees it and she's like, "Heyyyy, I wear a retainer too," and

I'm like, "It's not a retainer, it's a diaphragm." And then it's just a whole lotta awkward silence while she packs my bags.

Cervical Cap

Okay, I really didn't know what this was so I looked it up and according to Planned Parenthood, "The cervical cap is a silicone cup shaped like a sailor's hat." Ennnnh, wrong, F that. I am NOT putting anything inside me that looks like a sailor's hat. Hey look, it's Fleet Week in my vajayjay! Then again, if I were single and living in New York, I would totally wear this for Fleet Week. Damn straight I support the Navy, check out my cervi cap!

The Sponge

Blagggggggghhh, I feel gross just typing that word. Do I seriously need my birth control named after a cleaning product? I clean enough shit around here already. Plus, what the hell is the point of using a birth control that is only 80% effective? I shit you not. Twenty out of 100 women get preggers on the sponge. It's like Russian roulette in your hoo-ha. Only you don't die if you lose. It's worse. You have a crying, screaming, cockblocking, pooping baby.

So the other day my totally awesome husband sent me this text from work that said, "I love you." Awwwww. So I started to text him back, "I love you too." But adding the word "too" just kind of cheapened it in some way, like I wouldn't have said it if he didn't say it first, so I took off the word "too" and now it just said, "I love you," but that didn't seem like enough or something like I was just copying what he said, so I added an exclamation mark, "I love you!" But then it just sounded like I was yelling at him. And that's when it occurred to me that he's a guy and probably already forgot that he even sent me a text in the first place. Plus we've been married five years so finally I just texted back, "Can you pick up some milk on your way home?"

SOMETIMES I THINK LIVING IN HELL WOULD BE BETTER THAN THE SUBURBS

Here are the things I love about the burbs:
The storage space
My garage

And here are the things I HATE:

1. Before I got married and had kids and became a lamewad, I made fun of people who went to places like Applebees and Noodles and Company. My husband and I swore we'd never become THOSE people. Why the hell would you waste your money on crappy food in a shitty atmosphere being served by people who have to fake smile and pretend like they like you? And now I know. Kids. They change everything. But what sucks about the burbs is that we all go to these places alllll the time and over time our bar gets lower and lower and lower. So we say things like, "Have you been to that new Italian joint? It's pretty good." And what we mean is it's not pretty good, but their highchairs have clips that work and the food isn't poisonous and the employees aren't going to stab you with eye daggers if your kid licks the tops of all the parmesan cheese shakers.

2.   Ever drive by a suburban mall at eight in the morning and there are all these cars parked there and you're like did the stores open early or something? Ennhh wrong. Just step inside and you'll see who's there. Walkers. Nooo, not like the awesome zombie walkers on The Walking Dead. These walkers are way lamer and wayyy scarier. It's like the AARP organized a Flash Mob and convinced every old person in the area to meet at the mall to exercise. They strap on their whitest tennies, drop their coats in one of the "lounge" areas (aka places men wait and then fall asleep while their wives shop) and then they all walk. Around and around and around and around and around and around like F'ing gerbils on one of those wheel thingies. Hey, there's that Coach bag I like. Hey, there's that Coach bag I like again. Hey, and it comes in green too. Hey, there's that Coach bag I want. And they know shit like "from Gymboree to The Gap" is an eighth of a mile.

3.   When you live in the burbs you see your neighbors like every day but you don't know half their names. When we first moved here like 5,000 neighbors stopped by to introduce themselves because that's what weirdos, uhh people in the burbs, do (unlike the city where people know that nothing good can come from knowing your neighbors because you live so close together you can hear each other having sex and fights and stuff). So they all stopped by to meet us, only I have this condition called IA (Introduction Amnesia), so I can't remember any of their names now. My husband and I have had a three-year debate over whether the man across the street is Chip or Rich, so we just call him Chip-Rich which makes me hungry for an ice cream sandwich every time I say it. And it sucks when he's leaf-blowing at like zero o'clock in the morning and I want

to yell at him out the window. I guess I could just yell, "Chip or Rich, shut the F up!" Or "Yo fuckwad," but that's what city neighbors do across air shafts, not suburban neighbors across the street. Plus, he's kind of nice and I see him like six times a day.

4. Okay, I know all the burbs aren't like ours, but I haven't seen a black person in months. Wait, that's not true, we watched The Princess and the Frog the other night. But in all seriousness, this sucks. I know they're a minority, but according to our area, they're either nonexistent or invisible. So when I'm watching Sesame Street with my kids, I'm always like, "Look there's a black person!" or, "Hey, she's Indian!" And this is wrong for so many reasons.

5. Here's the kind of shit you get excited about when you live in the burbs. A house down the street is going on sale!!! I shit you not. The other day I was driving down the street and I saw a *For Sale* sign and I got all pumped up. Why? I have no F'ing idea. It's like 23 houses away from ours and has no bearing on my life whatsoever. I'm like ooooh, maybe a young family will move in. Well, I have no clue who lives there right now and for all I know a young family already lives there. And then one day a few weeks later I'm driving and the sign is gone and a moving truck is there, and I'm like stalking the movers to see what kind of shit they're hauling inside. Hmmm, that looks like an old lady table and I get all disappointed, but then I drive by an hour later and see a sandbox and I'm all excited again! And then they move in but I never meet them because they live 23 houses away. But that was exciting! Not.

6.	Okay, here's another stupid thing you get excited about living in the burbs. The mail arriving. I shit you not again. For two years now I've thought about WD40'ing my squeaky mailbox, but thank God I never get around to it because that squeak means MY MAIL IS HERE! What am I, an F'ing dog? I swear if I could bark and run around the living room I would. And for what? Bills and a bunch of catalogs I never look at like Oriental Trading (isn't that politically incorrect? It sounds like we're slave-trading Asians) and Everything Jewish (yes, that's a real catalog, but I've never actually opened it so for all I know the pages are blank).

7.	When I lived in the city and like 8 million neighbors could see in my window, for some reason I didn't give a rat's ass if they saw my ratty ass. But as soon as you live in a house with a ground floor, you can no longer walk around naked. Yeah, that's right. I'm a nudist. Not really, but you know what sucks? When your kid is screaming for milk but you're blow drying your hair naked because it's too F'ing hot to put on a robe, and the only way you can get the milk in the kitchen is to either put something on and sweat and ruin your hair, or do what I do. I basically cover up as much as I can with my hands and run downstairs as fast as I can past the window turning my backside to it, which isn't really a good option since it's pretty much as bad as my front side, if not worse. And all the time I'm hoping and praying that Chip-Rich isn't watching. Your driveway might be clean Chip-Rich, but your view is dirty dirty dirty.

8.	Did you know that when you live in the burbs, you can choose to never go outside? Like here's what I did today. Woke up and checked my temperature on my weather app. Drove my kid to school and they took her out of the car for me. Stopped at the drive thru bank and drive thru pharmacy on the way home (why the hell is that word spelled *thru* and not *through*?). Waited for the Peapod delivery that came right in the front door. Went to a play date at my friend's, but she lives over six houses away so of course we drove. Seriously, NEVER WENT OUTSIDE. So the other day when my doctor suggested I start taking Vitamin D and I was surprised, she asked me if I get outside much. Uhhh yeahhh, every time I walk from the car into Tarjay. Duh.

Oh yeah, that reminds me. I forgot one thing I do love about the burbs. Living so close to TARJAY!!!!!!! (insert angels singing here) And thank God I have all that storage space in my house so I have somewhere to put all the shit I don't need but I buy anyway there.

So I know when I see news stories about polygamists I'm supposed to think they're all crazy and shit, but secretly I'm a little jealous and kind of want my own sister wives. I know that's a little weird but:

1. I don't think it would be such a bad thing to have the bed to myself a few nights a week. Hello covers all to myself, goodbye fart smells that singe my nose hairs.

2. It'd be nice to share the nagging with someone else around here. "Did you nag him about the toilet seat yet because I just nagged him about the trash?"

3. I'd be REQUIRED to wear full-coverage skirts and tops every day. Adios cankles and flabby arms.

4. "Mommy Mommy Mommy Mommy!" Yo sister wife, I think our whiny rug rat is looking for you.

5. Hells yeahhhh, someone to dump my kids on while I go food shopping (translation: get my nails done).

6. I'd be expected to wear a ponytail every day! EXPECTED TO! Like I'm breaking a rule if I don't wear one. Sign me up!

Holy crap, have you been to a restaurant where "kids eat free" on a Sunday night. WTH did I just step into? MAD chaos. Like it felt like we were eating spaghetti in an F'ing mosh pit. At one moment my childless sister looked around and I heard her mutter to herself, "This is not what I want in life." No shit Sherlock. None of us ever wanted THIS. In fact, I think it should be mandatory that ALL teenagers go on a tour of this restaurant on a Sunday night. 'Cause there ain't no better birth control on the market.

MINIVANS ARE THE AWESOMEST! (NO THAT WHOLE TITLE IS NOT A TYPO)

So you know where I am right now? I'm sitting in the stupid Starbucks parking lot typing this. Yup, on the way home from dropping off numero uno at school, numero doso fell asleepo in the caro on the way homo (wait, that's not right), and since he has music class at ten, I'm letting him nap while I sit in the parking lot stealing Wi-Fi from Starbucks. Yes, I'm that loser. But hey, my son gets in his nap so he isn't a raging a-hole in music class. At least not because he's tired. If he is, it's because I forgot to give him a snack or change his diaper or accidentally zipped his skin up in his zipper or something.

But it's kind of appropriate that I'm typing this from my car because today as I was leaving my kid's school one of the other moms asked me a question.

OTHER MOM: So I've been meaning to ask you something. How do you like your minivan?

Hmm, how do I like my minivan?

ME: I *LOVE* it!

Errrrrrrrrrrr! In case you're wondering, that's the sound of tires coming to a screeching stop. WTF???!!! Did the L word seriously just leave my mouth?! And then it occurred to me, holy shit, I really do love my minivan. How depressing is that?!

So here goes. If I don't slit my wrists before I get to the end of this, here are 7 reasons why I love my minivan:

1.   Question: How may cup holders does a mom need? Answer: Infinity. Water bottles, sippy cups, coffee cups, old sippy cups with DIY cottage cheese, snack cups, drive-thru cups, Happy Meal toys, other shit, yada yada yada. There are like a million and a half things I put in the cup holders in my car. And my minivan has 12, count'm, TWELVE cup holders! THIRTEEN if you count the one in my kid's car seat. Yup, a baker's dozen in less than 100 cubic feet. Damn, now I'm craving a donut.

2.   "Make it stop! Make it stopppppppp!" my kid used to yell from the backseat of my old car like her eyes were being fried by an F'ing laser. Well guess what kiddo. Despite how amazing you think I am, at least until you're a teenager and think I'm the biggest loser (and not in a good Jillian Michaels kind of way), despite how all-powerful you think I am, I cannot turn off the sun. So unless you just want to keep driving east until we plunge into the freezing waters of Lake Michigan and die, the sun is going to shine in your window and in your eyes. So thank F'ing Buddha (since this car was made in Japan) my minivan comes with those totally awesome built-in shade thingies so the sun won't burn her eyes out anymore.

3.   There are many days I would like to steamroll my child flat but restrain myself, so hell if I'm gonna let someone else have the pleasure. Which is why probably my favorite feature EVER is the electric sliding doors. Alls I have to do is push a button and the doors open up like magic so she's not running around the parking lot like a Tasmanian devil. Instead she's in the car digging through the center console for my tic tacs so she can dump the entire contents into her mouth at once, except for that one little sucker that jams itself in the box sideways so you can't get it out unless you whack the crap out of the box on your steering wheel.

4.   I don't know about you but after a long ass day I like to wind down with some good old-fashioned music, and since I NEVER get the car to myself anymore, the kids are always there to hear it. Two Live Crew. Eminem. Easy E. All the crap that Walmart won't sell that helps me decompress. So you know what I'm thankful for? That little button I push on the minivan stereo that instantly turns off the music in the back seat. Sometimes when I'm feeling extra motivated I let the kids listen, but I push the button every time there's a swear word. Hells yeah, I'm as powerful as the FCC! Take that Janet Jackson's nipple!'

5.   Do you know what's awesome about having a third row of seats? That I can drive around other people's rug rats too. *NOT.* I always wonder why in God's name people literally buy an extra car seat to schlep around someone else's child. Oh yes, please give me one more set of vocal cords that'll make me want to chop my ears off while I'm driving. But you know what that third row of seats *is* good for? Ever since DSS told us we can't prop Holden's eyes open with toothpicks to keep him

from falling asleep, one of us sits back there when we want to keep him awake on the way home. Because some kids are good with the transition to bed. And some kids suck balls.

6.   OMG, did I seriously forget this one? The fact that I can get into the minivan myself while I'm strapping my kid into her car seat is AWESOME. Because when there's a tornado outside and it's like negative 100 degrees and the car seat straps are twisted like a thousand times, it's oh so nice to be inside the vehicle.

7.   This is how the saleslady explained how to fold up our stroller. "You just press this little button, go like this and presto it collapses and you can fit it in the palm of your hand." And this is how I sound when I'm actually doing it. "Mother-fucker, goddamned piece of shit for a stroller that sucks ass." And then I'm standing there in the parking lot with my stroller that won't collapse or fit into a trunk. Until… voila, the third row of seats folds down in a jiffy and I can just roll that bad boy right in totally erect. Okay, do I hear someone laughing? Yes, I said the word erect. What are you in the third grade? Yeah me too, erect erect erect! Tee hee hee.

So there you go. A bunch of reasons why I love my minivan. Maybe I'll buy a bumper sticker that says *I love my minivan* and then I'll put it on my minivan. But only if it's one of those magnetic ones because I wouldn't want to mess up my minivan with a sticker. Because I love it.

You know you've been married a long time when:

1.   *Your maiden name starts to sound weird to you.*

2.   *You can say words like vagina and clitoris to your husband without flinching.*

3.   *You're not mortified when he walks in on you waxing your mustache.*

4.   *As you're walking out of the room you accidentally crop-dust it with a series of audible toots and you don't even pause.*

5.   *You can donate his clothes you don't like without asking. Not that I do that, honey.*

6.   *You'll openly admit when your hemorrhoid is flaring up.*

7.   *You ask him to buy tampons for you and all he says is "Which kind?"*

8.   *You're a-okay with your thigh fat spreading out on the seat when you're wearing a bathing suit and sitting next to him.*

9.   *Your husband brings you to the toilet to show you how big his turd is. And then when you make a big one, you're tempted to show him. You don't, but the thought does cross your mind.*

10.   *You're not embarrassed when he walks in on you tipping your head back and squirting whipped cream directly into your mouth from the bottle.*

11. *You can say, "Not tonight honey, I'm not in the mood."*

12. *You can say, "Not tonight honey, I have a yeast infection."*

13. *You can say, "Not tonight honey, we already did it this month."*

14. *You can tell him you have diarrhea.*

15. *You can pick up your phone, a book, and a magazine and walk into the bathroom and tell him you might be a while.*

16. *If you pop a zit and it won't stop bleeding, you can put a little piece of tissue on it and walk around the house with it.*

17. *You're no longer worried that when he lifts the blanket he's going to be hit with your giant fart cloud.*

18. *When you shower with him, you can tell him to move over so you can blow a snot rocket.*

19. *You watch TV on different TV sets sometimes so you can each watch the shit you want to.*

20. *You stop swallowing.*

Hey if you have to, go ahead and flush twice, honey. Don't think of it as wasting water. Think of it as saving your wife's eyeballs.

Yo Rug Rats, You Owe Me $26,000 For Plastic Surgery

ALLLLLLLL THE WAYS MY BODY IS DIFFERENT (AKA SUCKS BALLS) AFTER CARRYING TWO POOP MACHINES

So here's the thing. We all have some part of our body that we've always wanted to change. I imagine even supermodels do. Granted it's their brain, but it's something (awww shit, I just offended all the supermodels reading this. All zero of them. I mean it's not like supermodels can read. I'm kidding, I know they can but I say mean things because I'm jealous of them). Anyways, the body part I want to change is my thighs. I mean, really it's that whole lower body region (zip code 60024), but if I had to pick just one specific part it'd be my thighs.

By the way, what totally sucks is while I'm writing about my excessive thighs, I keep going to the kitchen to get more turkey jerky. Damn you Costco and your giant bags of shit I don't need to eat. I'm eating it now as opposed to later at my OST (Official Snack Time) so my husband's not subjected to my turkey jerky breath tonight. Oh, who the F am I kidding? You know he's going to get home later and be like, "Were you eating turkey jerky?" Uhhh, yeah, like four hours ago. That shit lingers.

But I digress. A lot. So here's what really sucks balls. When you get preggers you don't get to pick which body part you carry your little poop machine in. 'Cause if I got to pick, I'd totally pick my thighs. Why ruin a perfectly good body part like my somewhat concave belly when my thighs are already beyond repair?

Which leads me to the point of this. Yes, there is a point. The top nine ways being preggers destroyed some perfectly good body parts of mine. Yes, nine:

1.	So you've heard of a FUPA right? For those of you who don't know what that is, just Google it. Wait, no, that's like when I used to ask my mom what a word meant and she'd be like, "Go look it up," and goddamn it, I'm not old enough to say shit like that yet. A FUPA is a (whisper this part) fat upper pussy area. Blaggggh, I feel like I have to go take a shower now. Anyways, now that we got that shit out of the way, ever since I had two babies, I have a FUPA. Which totally sucks because I used to only have an UPA. Man, I really miss my UPA. How the F do I get rid of the F and get my UPA back?

2.	WTH happened to my bladder? I mean, I totally get why it was a hot mess when I was preggers. That baby was in there leaning on it and kickboxing it and squeezing it like a sponge so I had to pee like every other second. But now the baby's out, so I don't get it. And it's not like my vajayjay's all stretched or something— I had a c-section. Makes no F'ing sense.

3.	Okay, you know when you find an old, mostly-deflated balloon in the toy bin and it's a little wrinkled because it used to be filled with air? Yeah, that's what my boobs look like now. Only they're not some fun color like red or purple. They're Caucasian-colored. (At first I wrote flesh-colored, but that's bullshit since flesh comes in like all different colors. Remember how Crayola used to have that peach crayon that was called flesh? Introducing the racist crayon! Wait, how did I go from deflated boobs to racist crayons?) Anyways, on a scale from one to ten my boobs used to be like a six and now they're like a three. On a good day. If that.

4. While we're on the subject of boobs, WTF happened to my nipples? Ever since I breastfed, they literally have wrinkles. I mean I look at them in the mirror now and I want to plug in my iron. And I don't even know if I own an iron. The next thing I know AARP is gonna start sending catalogs to our house addressed to Karen's nipples.

5. Ohhhh yeah, here's probably the worst one of all. My tush hole. No, not my front tush. I expected that shit to change. But my a-hole??? Yup, my a-hole gave me the most thoughtful baby shower present ever. A lovely hemorrhoid (why the hell is that word so hard to spell? All in favor of changing the spelling to hemroid, say aye!). I mean I'm not surprised I had one when I was preggers. I'd sit on the toilet for like hours on end trying to push out an F'ing rabbit turd, so it makes sense. But it's still here. Does this shit like NEVER go away?!!! And just when he hasn't reared (is that the right word???) his ugly head for a while and I think maybe he's gone, he pokes his fat head out again and he's like, "Hello, Karen!" And yes, I'm sure he's a he. He even starts with the letters "he." I kind of picture him like Newman on Seinfeld.

6. Okay, my feet are so small, sometimes I think it's a miracle that I'm not constantly falling over. I'm like the opposite of a Weeble Wobble. So you'd think I might be happy that my feet

grew like half a size during my second pregnancy. Ennnhhhh, wrong. It doesn't sound like a big deal until you consider the fact that I have an entire closet of shoes that DON'T F'ING FIT ANYMORE. So now every time I get dressed up for a night on the town (all two times we've gone out since having kids), I'm like Anastasia trying to cram her grotesque foot into Cinderella's glass slipper.

7. I don't have bags under my eyes. I have luggage sets. And it doesn't seem to matter how much beauty sleep I get. I swear sometimes it looks like two caterpillars are camped out under the skin beneath my eyes, and I totally wouldn't be surprised if my skin opened up one day and two butterflies flew out. I might be a little freaked out, but mostly I'd be psyched to get rid of my bags.

8. Before I was preggers I only pictured muffin tops on those slutty high school chicks who wear super low, low-rise, thong-showing jeans with short shirts. And now I stand corrected. I could wear pants up to my diaphragm, but as soon as I button them closed my extra skin would just cascade out all over the waistband. Like if it's raining outside and someone forgets their umbrella they should just duck under my overhangs.

9. Okay, I don't know if my uterus is all annoyed that she's being ignored after getting all that attention for 9 months, but this is what my period used to be:

.

And now it's:
!!!!!!!!!!!!!!!!

Uty (that's my uterus' nickname) is all like, "Yeah, you know how you were all psyched and shit not to have your period for fifteen months? Well, I saved up all that junk for you and now I'm gonna deliver it." The first time I got my period after breastfeeding I was like, "Agggghhhhh, I'm bleeding to death, call 911!"

So that's nine, and I'm too lazy to write more even though there are so many more things to bitch about. Baby brain, stretch marks, varicose veins, your pee spraying everywhere, etc. etc. etc. Oh and I'm sure the women who had vaginal births probably have plenty more to add, but I ain't gonna go there. Every time that comes up, half of my friends say their vajayjays are tighter than the eye of a needle while the other half claim their vajayjays are like gaping Grand Canyons or some shit like that. Eww gross. I mean, uhhh, all vaginas are beautiful.

SOME A-HOLE AT PANERA: Congratulations! When are you due?

ME: Twenty months ago, fuckface. It's called a muffin top.

FYI, I didn't really say fuckface, but I totally wanted to.

CROTCH AND OTHER WORDS THAT MAKE ME UNCOMFORTABLE

You know those skinny bitches who can order jeans off the Internet that they've never tried on before and when they arrive they fit perfectly? I am not one of them. And if you're one of them, I'm sorry for calling you a bitch, as well as a lot of other names behind your back.

I'm one of those d'Anjou-shaped women who goes to the store and apologizes to the salesperson 9,000 times for bringing 100 pair of jeans into the fitting room. And then after trying on all of them, I'm forced to pick between the pair with the acid wash and the pair with factory-made holes because they're the only ones I could squeeze over my thighs.

Where am I going with all of this? Well, the other day I went shopping with my mom at my third favorite store in the whole wide world.

#1. Tarjay
#2. Costco when they put out the free samples
#3. Nordstrom, where they'll let you return anything, even shit you didn't buy there. Except toddlers (yes, once I tried)

So anyways, I'd vowed not to shop for new jeans until I dropped most of the baby weight I'd gained, but A. I'm coming to realize that ain't gonna happen, and B. Every time I lean over I'm petrified someone is going to notice that I'm still wearing maternity jeans. So F it.

As I'm standing in the fitting room in a mountain of discarded jeans that must be mislabeled with the wrong sizes, I try on the last pair. Hello, what is this? A pair that fits? They're perfect. Ahhhhhhhhhhhh (FYI, that's the sound of angels singing). The color, the waist, the rise, the crotch (almost as bad as the words *moist* and *kumquat*). I look at the label. NYDJ. Hmm, what does that stand for?

And then it hits me. Not Your Daughter's Jeans. Oh no you di'n't. I can't buy these. Isn't *Not Your Daughter's Jeans* just a fancy way of saying MOM jeans? True, I do have a daughter of my own now and I don't want to wear her jeans, but only because they're covered in residual poop particles after giant poopie diapers. As I stand there staring at my finally perfect looking ass, I wonder whether it's worth it. Should I buy a pair of Mom jeans?

Well, let's just say if you see me looking awesome in a pair of jeans, you're welcome to whistle at my sexy tush. Just don't ask me why the label is scratched off.

I kind of wish sexting was around when I was a teenager because I'd really like a commemorative picture of what my boobs used to look like.

40 IS THE NEW "I WANT
TO KILL MYSELF"

Anyone who knows me well knows I have FIBS. Fake Irritable Bowel Syndrome. It tends to flare up when a new People Magazine arrives (courtesy of my MIL who passes me her old ones because I'm too cheap to subscribe).

ME: Honey, can you watch the kids while I go to the bathroom for a few minutes?

TRANSLATION: I've got a date with some hot celebrities who just had babies but already look great in bikinis and make me feel like shit.

So yesterday I opened up my two-week-old People magazine and found an article titled "40 is the new 20." And since I'm turning 40 tomorrow (unless someone is nice enough to pour me a cup of Drano), I thought how F'ing appropriate. I think to properly pick this shitty article apart, we should start at the beginning. The title. 40 is the new 20. I sure as hell hope not. Here's what I was doing when I was 20:

1. Walking home with my undies inside out after a stupid ass frat party.

2. Telling people I didn't think email would ever catch on because people like to hear each other's voices.

3. Hovering over a public toilet puking up pink daiquiri (thank you spell check) as my roommate held my hair back and in between vomits I apologized as it splattered all over our naked calves. I owe you my firstborn, Hannah. No seriously, come take her. At least until she's five. And then again when she's a teenager.

So if 40 is the new 20, kill me now. I want nothing to do with it. But just for shits and giggles (BEST. PHRASE. EVER.) let's continue on to what some of the celebs are saying about being 40.

Sofia Vergara bitches about her thrice-weekly (is thrice even a word 'cause it sounds made up) torturous glute workouts, but adds that the results are totally worth it. Ennhh, wrongo. I'm calling bullshit on this one Sofe. You don't look like that because of your workouts. You look like that because of some damn good genes. I could work out *thrice* a day for two years straight and my glutes would still look pregnant.

And Jennifer Garner says, "I'm really happy. I'm in a great place in my life." Oh yeah, which place is that? Your home in LA, New York, France or Bali? I'm just making that shit up but I imagine that's where she has homes. Yeah, I'd be in a good place too if I had multiple mansions, and none of that McMansion shit. Not that I have anything against McThings. Oh shit, now I have a craving.

And then there's Gwenyth (how the F do you spell that name?!) Paltrow's page. She says a lot of good stuff, but then ends it with, "After two kids I look better now than I did when I was 22." Ehhhh, wrong! You look good G. You'd look good at 80 wearing a paper bag, but you don't look better than you did at 22. No F'ing way. The only reason you might think that is because you probably had some weird haircut or were wearing a lame flannel shirt in the mid 90's, but there ain't no way your belly looks better AFTER you had two kids.

Oh and I LOVE what Gabrielle Union says about staying beautiful. "I drink a gallon of water a day." A gallon?! A. I'd have to duct tape a water bottle to my mouth to drink that much. And B. I'd have to duct tape a toilet to my tush.

Anyways, blah blah blah, the article goes on and on and I need to stop talking about it because I'm just sounding like a jealous bitch. Which I am. Because I'm pretty damn sure when it comes to MY body, 40 is NOT the new 20. Unless of course when I was 20 I had a muffin top, a beard, an F'ing constellation chart on my chest, extra elbow skin like a friggin' elephant, and boobs that belong on the cover of National Geographic.

To achieve Baby Sideburns'
look of the week

Worry about the following to attain lustrous gray hair overnight: choking, electrocution, bullying, impalement, Ebola, and every other F'ing thing you can imagine

Use Mother Nature's conditioner (grease) to pull back hair in a ponytail daily

Apply a daily facemask of spit-up and sailva

Don't get a full night of sleep for 3.5 years

Drink crazy amounts of brown caffeinated drinks

Wash face as little as possible to attain adult onset acne

Wipe armpits with baby wipes on non-MSD's (Must Shower Days)

Do your boobs hang low,
Do they wobble to and fro,
Can you tie them in a knot,
Can you tie them in a bow,
Did your little poop machine suck all the life out of them
and leave them to look like tube socks filled with sand
with nipples you could use in the ring toss game at a carnival,
Do your boobs hang low?

Yeah, maybe it's not as good as the original,
but hell, neither are my boobs.

I just sneezed like ten times.
Which basically means I just peed myself like ten times.

AN OPEN LETTER TO MY VAJAYJAY

Warning: the following letter is full of gross language, a lot of F words and crap men don't want to hear. And you know if *I'm* warning you, this shit's gonna be bad. Just sayin'. Still here? Okay then, here we go.

Dear Vajayjay,

We've been together for a long time now, so I feel like I can be honest with you. WTH happened? You used to be my trusted little gal but ever since I had the kiddos you've really let yourself go.

I used to be able to put down like a keg of beer and you'd "hold it" until I was up to my eyeballs in urine, but now I can barely get through the intro to Modern Family without soiling the sofa. Thank God for microfiber, right? I'm telling you, the person sitting next to me sneezes and a little sneaks out of me. WTF?

And here's the thing, Gina, I don't get it. Can we just pause for a moment here and ask who chooses to name their daughter Gina? It's literally the nickname for vagina. But I digress.

Let's just say for the sake of this discussion that I didn't have two C-sections and that I actually shot two 8-pound bowling balls out my hoo-ha like Mother Nature intended. It's not like I had my babies through the pee hole and it got all stretched out or something.

And that's kind of beside the point anyways because I didn't even have them through you. I got my damn FUPA sliced open so they could airlift those babies out of me. Is *that* what this is about, Vaj? You're pissed at me because I didn't use your F'ing birth canal? I've got one word for you: episiotomy. Or as I like to call it, cutting your vagina open with a pair of scissors. Here are five more words for you: Holy F'ing shit that hurts.

Anyways, let's pull it together here. I'm 40, you're 40, we're not F'ing senior citizens yet. I refuse to buy Depends until I'm at least 65 (now if some angel out there were to drop off a box on my porch, I'm not saying I'd be totally against it, especially for situations like long car rides and county fairs that only have porta potties with names like Oui Oui).

So pull your shit together (can I say that to a vajayjay?). If that means you've got to do some kegels once in a while, go for it. I may not have time to exercise, but that doesn't mean you can't. 'Cause if you don't start doing a better job I'm putting in a catheter. A big ole unlubricated one made out of sandpaper. Oh yeah, spell check, then how the F do you spell unlubricated? It's just lubricated with un on the front of it. Duh.

And if that's not incentive enough, V, how's this for a threat? Hold my pee in from now on or I'm pulling out the big guns. Yup, say adios to your favorite vibrating toy. I'm taking out the double A's and putting them into some lame ass remote control downstairs. And not a cool one like the universal remote.

Don't you queef at me. I'm serious. Oh shit, I think I just crossed a line. Yes, even I have a line.

Love and kisses,
The bitch that owns you

THE END

Holy crap, did you seriously read this whole book?! Thank you! You deserve a gold medal or something. Yeah, seriously.

How to claim your prize:

1. Go to your kid's art supplies.

2. Find some yellow construction paper.

3. Cut out a round circle and write the words "gold medal" on it.

4. Find a safety pin and attach it to your shirt.

5. Clean up the construction paper before your kid sees it and wants to do some F'ing art project that's all messy and shit and will require lots of help from you and that you'll have to put up on the fridge even though it SUCKS ASS until a few days have passed and you can bury it at the bottom of the trashcan when your kid's not looking.

6. Wear that shitty gold medal with pride and if someone looks at you weird tell them to F off and respect your ass because Baby Sideburns gave it to you.

ACKNOWLEDGMENTS

Thank you to my amazing husband who has always supported me in everything I do, even when it's terribly embarrassing.

Thank you to my parents whose love and support has gotten me to where I am today.

Thank you to Lyssa Bowen who illustrated this book hilariously, and who took my endless comments like a champ.

And a HUGE-ASS (is that hyphenated? I'm not sure) THANK YOU to the people who supported my Kickstarter project. Without your help, I would never have been able to complete my lifelong dream of writing this book. I hope you like it.

And here is a special shout out to some of those awesome supporters (in no particular order). Thanks so much:

Domestic Goddess Crystalyn Huegen
Mini Boss of the Walter Household: Princess Zoe Rose
The best and most perfect and wonderful Gramma of Princess Serene, Susan Breding
Queen Doodlebug & Sir Tunkabutt McCormick
Neighbor For Life Stacey Slater (you know it sister!)
Erin "I-Wish-I-Lived-Next-Door-To-Baby-Sideburns" Pauls
Supernurse Sandy Hall

Mommy Mojo

Lisa Dwyer-Edison

JayDee

Sarah Holbrook Bolding (whose new name looks fabulous)

Grandma Cindy Alpert, who's awesome for lots of reasons but especially because she gives me all of her People magazines

Katelyn & Hannah Tarnoff (two of the sweetest sisters on earth)

Bladerunners Vince, Isabel & Eric

Her Royal Canadian Majesty, Quinn Wyse

Lady Jennifer L. Campbell

Erin (The down-trodden servant to a house full of boys)

Abby Robinson

Kristin Gaspe Girl McCallum

Valerie "Scrunchies Forever" Mazzelli

Kamila Starzynski

Tracy "Toys" Donaldson

The Boy, Jelly Donut, and Baby Morea! (CIA)

ApeBro

saucyabby

Andrea Griffiths

Roberto+Natasha=MaverikDustinChad Mannino

Ashley Endicott

Lauren NeverAMomentToMyself McEwen

Karen Last, Tribe Leader

The Kwimmers

Lady Leigh Whiting

Melissa Hodge ... Evalina's momma <3

Sandra "Supermom" Lott

Lucyna Mackay Esquire

Deborah (you know!)...The Queen

The Mrs. Bradshaw

Mother Mad Scientist Lobdell
Kara Hoffmann Yako
Aisha Haiyoom
Jana Banana Warmiak
Angie Creasy
Barb "the best Aunt in the world" Santi
Alice Gomstyn, a.k.a. Mildly Inappropriate Mommy
The LindaDaveRonniJoshCamilleBrownieScampersCinnamon Clan
Bon "theboyzmom" Camm
Allison Larsson-Venello
Lori Farrell Magnificat
Timi Dury Williams
Lindsy Truitt
Shannon Mullen
Sabrina "The Real Housewife of Beaverton" Gonzales
Awesome Queen Jessica Princess Kayla Madison Megan
Mandy Mae Flower
Shelly Schitzerpantz
Her Most Awesomeness Stacy Scanlon
Julie "Sparty Alligator" Peacock
Ari Pie & Lukie Bug
Slucas Ü
Kelly Ain't No Plain Jane Smith
Natasha Anderson
Kim Radich
The amazing Kat Zisa
The Fabulous Myra McKinley
Samantha Nicole Schwarz
Peruvian Princess
Alli Esker
The Lytle Girls

Ilene Naddeo

Mackenzie from Raising Wild Things blog (www.raisingwildth-ings.com)

Julie De Guzman

April "Fiona" Kelly

L K Creekmur

Christine "Hot Mama" DeRosa

Courtney Bridwell

Michele & Princess Emily O'Connell

Samoan Queen Saleena Ghanny

Linda Drake

Amy Gers, who is always a source of inspiration

Jimmy, Robyn and Jase Maass

Princess Mia Amada Ramos

Jill Capolupo and Max Allen

Lori/Emma Petrillo

Camille Brashears the Incredible

Amber Harney

Jenny, CEO Team Dickinson

Supermom Erin Telford

Debra *The Lyrical Gangsta* Hudelson

Mother of Gus and Lanie

Beth Hannah

JKWhite

Her Royal Momminess, Michele Suerdieck

Gena Marie Lisanti

Mary Block

4x4 Wheelin' - Mud Luvin Coley

Mrs. LaLa Glitterbug

Optimistic Explorers William & Brady Shelor

Maria D. Walker

Piper Poppyseed Lageman
Team Criniti
Jennifer Williams
Jedi Master Potter Mandi
Kris Brownfield...mama of triplets and quads!
My Favorite Board Certified Lactation Consultant Ellen H. Schwerin
@ www.happymilk.us
Jack and Brady's Mommy
Fabulous Foster Families Everywhere!
Jana Fitzpatrick
Kung Pow Tracy
Colly Wolly Ding Dong / Colls Balls Meyers
Alicia Maloney
Kelly and Baby Barret
Supermom Robin Michon (able to read funny books in a single Poise
Pad)
Henry Thwaites the incredible!
Tricia (aka Maddie, Ian and Charlottes mom) McLister
The Domestic Project Manager--Kali Sakai
Her Lady of Snarkishness, Mandy Butka
Jennifer Hoppe
Westfir Stallion
Carri Sweeney, a.k.a. Wordy Nerdy Thirtyish
Leslie White - Daughter of Scary Evil Dragon Snake Queen
The Royal Callahan Family Of Grafton
Her Majesty Meagan Platt
Sue Landis, Queen of the Non-Sequitor
The wonderful, amazing Laura Prager-Diamond
Amy "Bug" Tillery
Amy Maitre Starkey
The Fabulous Nikkole Casper

Meagen Minor
Proud Poppa Jimmy Maass
Becky Bliefnick
The Lovely Coll Doll
Julie Terhune
Maureen Butler
Kelly 'ball of fucking joy' Mathews
Carissa Morin
Rachel Canuso Holt
Little Lady Corinne Garner
Katie Grim
Angie LaFountain Boyd
Supermom Kandi Alfredson
The Amazing Jennifer Lyn Travis
Pennapoo aka Bodhi's Mom
Charlie & Jack Konczal (and their mom who needs a nap and a martini)
Britt Kunz
Karen Green Pirinelli
The Gaboury's Sarah, Chris and Mason
K-Wex
Daniela Park
The amazingly awesome Haren and Kannah who didn't tell me to say she's amazing and awesome but she is so I am saying it
Queen of all the peppers, Kyla Elizabeth Allen
Adam Wellington Barney Yayyyy Taco!
Paula Jean Barney (Yanosy) Yayyyyy Taco's wife!
Lainey Bug Anderson
Olivia and Emma del Valle
Meaghan "I love both my kiddos bunches" Freeman
TT Mongoburger

Erin Hieber
Chelsea the Great!
Cavan and Emma's Mommy
Amy Lammert
Hockey Eh
Princess Grace Garrison
Ginger, mom of Christine and Ericka
Princesses Emerson & Ava Pontifex
Katy Wytko
Alexis Witt
Princesses Lolo Maddie Alyssa
Princesses Jill, Lele & Erica
My Special Kind of Crazy Mom
Mrs. Sylvester McMonkey McBean
Becky Reeves
Pam-a-rama ding dong
Laurie & Faith Hammancheeses
Sarah Cartwright
Amy Lazaro!!
Colleen Masotta
The Big Boss Sasha Paul
Jessica Gablin
Angela Elizabeth Moore
Amy Gailey
Reese & Macy's Mom
The Devine & Beautiful Linda Degelsmith
Liz "my Junior Mints always get stuck in the vending machine" Madison
linzie lewd
Kimberly Parolari
Doc Brown

Chief Snuggler Nina Bo Beena Duchin
Jackson & Hudson Coffman
Brenda Meller
Supreme stinkaponamous Amy MacDonald
HRH Stacy Barninger
Lauren 'LP' LaRoche
Warden Melissa Gizewski
Maryam Ghaznavi
The one and only Amanda Collins Berwitz
Beth Parker
Super Jackson and Princess Sabrina Lovas
Wildcat Liz
Queen of Everything Julieanna Ealley Scott
Melody Rose Shaw
Lesley, Madelyn & Cole Saxton
The Bermans (please move back to Chicago!)
Jess Grycko
the other Karen from HONO (HONO RULES!!!)
Gabs, Lola & Juju Muscatello
Crazy Cat Lady Liz Marsek
Colt and Walker Williams
Joanne the rockstar Rodgers
Hurricane Fritz-Waylon
The Moxie Chicks
Angie Princess of Bells
Tracy Fimple
Lauren (My Husband Was Pissed That I Bought A Book Before It
Was Completed) Danaher
Susie Prewitt
Hollandzilla's Mom
Miss "Aly Bug" Bungert

Cuchini.com ~ Say No To Camel Toe! ~ Our Lips Are Sealed!

JJD²

Amy Koenigsknecht

Lexi Newman

Bayou Belle of Baton Rouge, Katherine Hayes

D.T.F. Posko

James (Batman) Eisfelder and Cole (Robin) Eisfelder

Shauna "The Great" Mitchell

The Rabin Family

Miss Lauren mother of the year Baker!

The Honorable Jessica Byrne-York

Karen Elizabeth Torri

Mom to Mackenzie and Alayna

Kourtnei Ramirez aka Everett's Publicist

Lindsay L. Teplesky

JenieRedhead Lightfoot

Jaime Tyler

Alethea, Craig, Hailey, Dylan and Shane Shapiro

Laurie Mueller

Queen Traci - ruler of all things nonexistent!

Genevievette "GEWEL" Walker-Lightfoot aka Giavrielle's Mom

Angie Geitner

Jenny Davis

ReaganStar

Lindsey "Miss Spartacus" Barnes

Graham & Harper's Momma

Heather Berkley

Carrie Conway

Charlene "The Flower" Estrada

Becki Ciavarella Darville

Lady Jennifer Stewart

Minions of Snoopy Bryce
Rebecca Barber
Erica Sollars
Elizabeth A. Upp
Ridge & Weston's Mommy
Teresa a/k/a T-Bird Miller
Tania Clasen
Mrs. Teresa Fay Somerville-Rader
Princess Smellie Ellie
Mommy BJ Crazyass Barnett
Lovely Leah Walker
Missee Sahib Anderson
Suburban Snowflake
Michelle Bouley aka Tubesocks
Christine Wolf
Annie Luepker
Laurie Coleman Frederick
Kelly Thomas
Jessica Dix
Ashley Holland
Julia McCullough Perreman
Lisette Venegas
Nyla Maxwell
Molly DuBois
Kasie Marie Durden
Abigail Anastasio
AnnetteCraig Allen
John Cox
Michelle Muir
Amber Light
Chrisandra Symonds

Mary Mande
Becky
Kimi Fragar Martin
Jenny Ryan
Amber Lowe Cichon
Adair Campbell
Traci Johnston
Jaimie Andrews
Brenda Miller
And last but certainly not least, Melissa Keneally